YEARS NOT WASTED
1940–1945

YEARS NOT WASTED
1940–1945

A POW's Letters and Diary

Keith Panter-Brick

The Book Guild Ltd
Sussex, England

The Book Guild Ltd
25 High Street,
Lewes, Sussex

First published 1999
© Keith Panter-Brick, 1999
Set in Times
Typesetting by Keyboard Services, Luton

Printed in Great Britain by
Bookcraft (Bath) Ltd., Avon

A catalogue record for this book is
available from the British Library

ISBN 1 85776 329 7

CONTENTS

FOREWORD

The letters and diary written by Keith Panter-Brick while a prisoner of war constitute a moving and compelling account of his experience. In March 1939, aged eighteen and believing in the need to stand up to Nazi Germany, he enrolled in the Territorial Army. Captured by the Germans in May 1940, he spent virtually the entire war in captivity, most of it in Poland.

The Panter-Brick story is especially gripping because it sheds light on the experience of ordinary soldiers who, under the Geneva Convention, were obliged to work for their captors, unlike officers. He and his fellow soldiers lived a life of virtual slave labour. We are told that it was not necessarily always one of unmitigated hardship. Changing circumstances played their part, as did opportunism. These were hard years but events are described in a philosophical vein, with reactions and emotions ranging from sadness to elation. The overall impression is that of a steady determination to get on with life regardless of oppressive circumstances. The book reveals a triumph of the human spirit as well as an indestructible optimism.

As the title of the book proclaims, the years 1940–1945 were not wasted years. It was while a POW that Panter-Brick grew to maturity. His letters and diary stand as a testament to intellectual progress and the power of religious faith. Although during the war itself he remained a non-believer, he recounts how his war-time experience initiated a process of enquiry, beginning with reflections on moral dilemmas encountered while a POW, that lead on to a study of philosophy at Oxford and, thereafter, through marriage and other encounters to his affirmation of the Catholic faith. He also became a scholar and teacher at the London School of Economics.

In January 1945, Panter-Brick was caught up in the retreat of the German Army on the Eastern Front. He contrasts his own long winter march out of Poland and across northern Germany with the fate of comrades who were overtaken by the Russian advance. They remained virtual prisoners of the Russians, pawns in the struggle for power in Poland, while Stalin, Roosevelt and Churchill argued about its future. He managed to escape from the march in early April and reach American lines. He arrived home before those liberated by the Russians three months earlier, and mourned that for the Poles there was no freedom.

Wm Roger Louis
Kerr Professor, University of Texas, Austin
and Fellow of St Antony's College, Oxford.

PREFACE

I spent most of World War II in Poland, as a prisoner of the Germans. If I now tell of the experience, it is for three reasons.

First, thank to letters and a diary, fortunately preserved, much of it can be told in the way it was recorded at the time. It differs, in this respect, from most other accounts which reconstruct the past from memory – 'a marvellous but fallacious instrument'.[1] A dramatised reconstruction reads well but I prefer the contemporary record. Although more pedestrian, it has the merit of presenting the reader with a picture which is more revealing because less selective and which is also undeniably authentic.

Of course, prudence dictates what a POW records at the time, in letters or in a diary. We assumed that our mail was censored yet had no means of knowing what would be censored. We were not given any guidelines, nor was there any feedback. In actual fact, a more important constraint than censorship was the need to reassure family and friends that life was bearable. I tried to strike a balance. I wanted, on the one hand, to be informative, for my letters were the only reliable

---

[1] How memory is apt to play false when traumatic experiences are recalled is examined by Primo Levi in *The Drowned and the Saved*, Michael Joseph, 1988. 'The memories which lie hidden within us are not carved in stone; not only do they tend to become erased as the years go by, but often they change, or even increase by incorporating extraneous features.'

ix

source of information about my health, my state of mind and indeed everything else. On the other hand, I had sometimes to disguise my true feelings and to avoid mentioning anything likely to cause distress. This was sometimes difficult as, for instance, when I was put on trial and sentenced to two months' detention for stealing some cheese. We were, in any case, rationed to two letters and four postcards a month, sometimes less, so there was nothing to be gained by taking up valuable space with tales of woe which, if not in fact censored, would only have distressed those at home. So I wrote as cheerfully as possible. Only one of my letters arrived home with parts blacked out by the German censor. Some letters never arrived but not, I think, because of censorship. Letters were in transit for so long – invariably about two months – and travelled by routes so precarious that some were bound to go astray.

I could be more frank in my diary. It is a strange fact that diaries were tolerated. They were not one of the items regularly confiscated whenever a search was under way. Indeed, one year, a diary was put on sale which bore on the outside cover the number of our prison camp, Stalag XXA. Thus, unless one wrote – unwisely – about clandestine activities, involving people other than ourselves, keeping a diary secret from the Germans was not a problem.

At first, I did no more than make a note of my mail, and two years elapsed before I began to record other matters. I have to thank my sister, who preserved all my home correspondence, that a reliable record exists for those early years and of the initial shock. Thereafter, through 1943 – an eventful year involving several changes of fortune – and 1944 – when I began to reflect more deeply on my experience – my diary provides an additional dimension. Finally in 1945, when all correspondence ceased, it was the only means of recording what was to prove the most anxious time of all, the long winter march out of Poland. By then, my diary – if that is the right word for the miscellaneous bits of paper – had become my most treasured possession, indeed my only possession apart from trousers and shirt, boots and greatcoat.

A contemporary record requires to be put into context and

needs occasional explanation. If something was prudentially not recorded – for instance, an escape – it must be reconstituted from memory. I have kept such additions to no more than is absolutely necessary, so that my letters and diary can tell their own story. My letters are quoted *in extenso*, only insignificant details, indicated by a line of dots, being deleted. My diary, when paper allowed it, is more verbose, so I have had to quote it more selectively. I have, however, omitted relatively little and nothing of substance.

Secondly, my account differs from many others not only in its form but also in its content. Most POWs were, like myself, privates. Lacking any rank whatsoever, we were put to work as is permitted in the Geneva Convention. Yet most accounts of POW life have been written by officers, who were under no such obligation. This makes a substantial difference. True, all of us, officers and men, experienced much the same boredom, homesickness, frustration and impatience, also the joy of receiving a long-awaited letter or Red Cross food parcel. But officers had to devise ways of occupying their time, whereas we privates were virtual slaves of the Germans. The one fate was not necessarily any worse than the other. They were simply different kinds of experiences.

How far apart they were from one another may be illustrated by the surprise with which I read the Rev. David Wild's book, *Prisoner of Hope*.[1] David Wild, an army chaplain taken prisoner in 1940, had renounced the right to be repatriated and had, moreover, chosen to attend to the spiritual needs of us men rather than to fellow officers. As he explains in his preface, it was on reading his own wartime notes that he realised that they presented 'a picture of POW life very different to that portrayed in many books of wartime reminiscences, most of which were about the experience of officer POWs'.

His own portrayal is none the less that of an officer. Although he was allowed to make brief visits to some of the

[1] Published in 1992 by The Book Guild.

xi

outlying work camps, his rank and the deference shown to him acted as a screen. He never really inhabited the world in which we were living. I had no idea, until I read his book, what a difference rank could make, even to a POW. I could not refrain from quiet chuckles on reading that he was accompanied on his visits by someone who carried his kit, that he usually sat down to a breakfast of bacon and eggs and that the guards did his bidding.

David Wild does admit that from his account one might conclude that 'life was not all that hard in German captivity'. He attributes it to the 'strange attachment' of Germans to what is 'correct', in this case, the Geneva Convention. He believed that the German Army (as distinct from the Gestapo and the SS) made a 'show of conforming most of the time to the requirements of the Geneva Convention'. Unfortunately for us privates, it required us to work and, while we were certainly spared the murderous brutality experienced by Polish and Russian prisoners, we were none the less open to exploitation. There were very few rules to which we could appeal whenever our employers and guards chose to treat us as slave labour. We were governed more by particular circumstances than by rules. There were times of hunger and times of plenty. There were times when we took care not to defy our guards and times when we could bribe them. We were sometimes exhausted and at other times we had energy to spare for all sorts of activities.

Thirdly, some of my letters and parts of my diary belie the general impression that the years spent as a POW were inevitably wasted years – years that served no purpose. Re-reading them, I appreciated, in retrospect, how valuable an experience it had been to me personally. Although they tell, most of all, of the boredom, of the monotony, of the drudgery and of the waste of time, there are moments of reflection and introspection which show that what seems to be a long interruption to purposeful life became in the end a revelation. Although I had little time of my own to study and gain some useful qualifications – this was an officer's privilege – I learnt a great deal about life, my fellow men and myself, especially myself. I grew up while I was POW. I was inclined at first to edit out from my letters and diary all my innermost thoughts but I would thereby have suppressed the most valuable part of the experience, to have presented it as a pure waste, and hence to have distorted the true story.

ACKNOWLEDGEMENTS

I was greatly encouraged and helped in the composition of this book by my academic colleagues, Professors Paul Jankowski, Roger Louis and John Watkins, by Mickie Watkins, and by my fellow POWs, Harold and Norman Marshall. I am indebted to Jane Pugh and Mina Moshkeri for the drawing of the maps.

The burden of writing was lightened considerably by the computer skills of my daughter Catherine, her husband Mark, and my granddaughter Alexandra. Catherine and Mark dealt most patiently with endless revisions and made many helpful suggestions. I thank my daughter Beatrice for her learned counsel.

1

All Set: False Start

It is easier, now that the 1939–45 war has receded into an earlier age, to share one's knowledge of it. Probably most have kept things to themselves, even from themselves. I refer, of course, not to exploits which one might jokingly recall, but to the knowledge, soon acquired once war has started, that the cost, in lives, in grief, in suffering, is immeasurable, and unacceptable however much one did accept it at the time.

I have only to look back on 1938–39 to see how easy and natural – and perhaps necessary – it is to respond to a call to arms. Like so many others, I accepted the need to stand up to Hitler and readily volunteered for part-time training. My preference was for the RAF Volunteer Reserve but I was told that there were no vacancies. Rather than remain on a waiting list, I joined the Territorial Army. My father had once been in the Cheshire Volunteers and I followed suit by enrolling in the Cheshire Regiment. A new 4th Battalion was being formed. Its A Company was filled almost entirely by men from my home town, Wallasey, except for the officers, for none of the schools in Wallasey boasted an Officer Training Corps.

I was 18 years of age at the time, and was perhaps following not so much my own considered judgement as my peers. Many of us who joined A Company had attended the local grammar school, had been Sea Scouts together and were members of the same tennis and rugby clubs. Putting on khaki was little more than a change of dress, the drill hall another venue for meeting one's friends, the summer camp not unlike those of the Scouts. The meagre pay was hardly a consideration.

Even when war came, little happened to set me thinking. For several weeks we remained near home, our social life continuing much as before. We started to miss home only when we were posted to the Berkshire Downs. We were put in stables said to have been condemned as unfit for horses. We had no greatcoats. I was exasperated by the waste of time and energy. Morning parade, when everything had to be spotless, was followed by endless gun drill in muddy countryside. The emphasis was put on practising indirect firing, the assumption – a false one – being that we were unlikely to have the enemy in our sights. My fondest memory of the time spent at Letcombe Bassett is a visit to Oxford, to see John Gielgud play in *The Importance of Being Earnest*.

After Christmas leave and a review by King George VI, we embarked for France, as part of the 48th Division. We gave the King three cheers but the thrice repeated order to lift one's cap and cheer made it sound hollow. Conditions in France were unbelievably bad. It was a very severe winter. We were billeted in a school, sleeping on the floor and having to wash at the pump outside. We used our dixies for both eating and shaving. The only really tasty food came from the local café, which served us innumerable plates of fried eggs and chips, and from the local cake shop, where my favourite delicacy was rum baba.

We became only slightly better acquainted with war in April 1940, which we spent entrenched some miles in front of the Maginot Line. We could sometimes see the enemy through binoculars but only the foot patrols, out at night in no man's land, risked coming into contact. One was more likely to encounter a booby trap in one of the houses which had all been evacuated. For weeks on end, we sat behind our Vickers machine-guns, and we were under strict orders not to disclose our positions by the slightest movement, let alone by opening fire. One night the guns of the Maginot Line let loose. There was, I believe, an enquiry the next day, for it was apparently all an expensive mistake, but a fine spectacle for us in the front line. When we left, the Lorraine countryside was a picture of peace, covered in fruit blossom.

The phoney phase of the war ended for us in mid-May. We had moved back to northern France, this time into more comfortable billets. We were supremely self-confident. We told the lady of the house not to worry about the German invasion of Belgium. We left some belongings with her saying that we would be back to collect them in due course. It was the 14th before we set out for Belgium, cheered on by the local population, and the 16th before we reached our allotted positions behind the river Dyle, which runs east of Brussels. That day Lord Gort, commander of the British Expeditionary Force, was ordered to withdraw to the line of the river Scheldt. Thus we had arrived only to turn around. For the next ten days the battalion was continually on the retreat until ordered to take up positions at Cassel, which had been General Foch's headquarters in 1914–15. There, not far from Dunkirk, survivors of the Cheshire, Oxfordshire and Buckinghamshire, and Gloucestershire battalions made a last-ditch stand.

Some of us had already been put out of action as early as 19th May. Our battalion, together with the 4/7th Royal Dragoon Guards, was spaced out behind the Dendre river, southwards of Lessines and north of Ath. Our orders were to hold the line until noon and then to withdraw. The morning was spent exchanging fire across the river but we were also worried by fire from closer to hand and from the rear. We had very little infantry in support. Civilians could be seen who might have been Germans in disguise or fifth columnists. One came into the farmyard where I was guarding the trucks. On seeing me, he vanished. At the appointed time, each platoon had to make its own way out. In anticipation of having perhaps to fight our way out, the guns had been mounted on the rear of the trucks, ready to fire. Driving the lead truck, I set off, the platoon commander, Second Lieutenant Williams, by my side. I think he expected me to know the way but we had arrived in darkness, had no maps and only knew that we had to make for

3

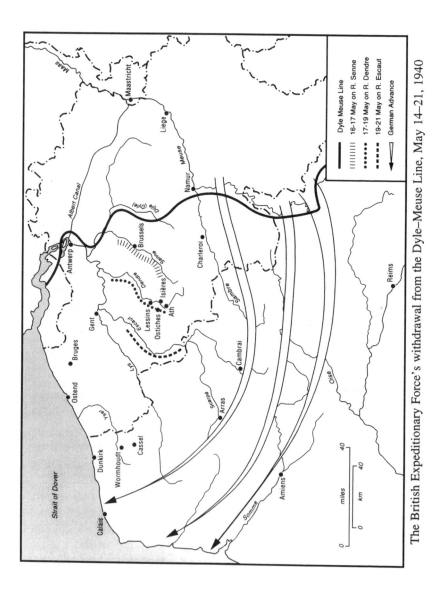

The British Expeditionary Force's withdrawal from the Dyle–Meuse Line, May 14–21, 1940

Ostiches. I was puzzled when stopped at a level crossing. The gate ran on wheels and had been pushed across the road as we approached. Nobody was to be seen. I got down, pushed it back and continued on my way. I stopped again when seeing, hidden in a ditch, someone in British uniform. He thought there might be some Germans ahead, but could give no more definite information.

After continuing not many yards more, we came under intense fire from somewhere on our left. Lieutenant Williams, sitting on my left, was killed in the first few seconds and his body rolled out on to the road. I kept going but no doubt braked instinctively as a grenade exploded right in front of me. The following truck crashed into mine and overturned. I was thrown out, or maybe I jumped out, on to the roadside. Weaponless, I lay still but, when I lifted my head to look around, I saw that a German already had me covered. Harold Marshall, who lay underneath the truck which had overturned, was relieved to see that I was being taken prisoner and not simply shot. All the other trucks had pulled up or been put out of action except the last in line. Although this truck managed to turn off and get away, one person on board was fatally wounded. It was George Shaw, the gentlest member of the platoon. We were herded down a side lane while some firing continued. Its high banks, covered in long grass, enabled me to get rid of my diary, which contained some information which might have been useful to the enemy. We waited, not sure that we were not going to be shot.

I have since read a 1943 German version of what had taken place that morning.[1] It makes unpleasant reading for it is written in triumph, but because it mirrors so exactly my own recollections and also reveals how we came to be ambushed, I found it fascinating. An advance party of the enemy's Seventh Infantry Division had reached Isières, on the other side of the river from us, in the early hours. The officer in command spied

---

[1] *Eine Infanterie Division Bricht Durch*, NSDAP, München 1943. This is not a German Army but a Nazi Party publication. Text by Paul Alverdes.

out the land from the church tower and from the top of the doctor's house. He spotted a stream leading to the river. It passed through dense bushes until it reached the river, at a point where this was no more than 20 metres wide. Two rubber inflatables were used to carry him and some of his men down the stream and across the river, while others provided a diversion by opening fire further along the river. Once across the river, the Germans, while waiting for reinforcements, dealt with whatever crossed their path. Two Bren gun carriers were put out of action, two dispatch riders killed and their messages read. One of the battalion's officers, Captain Lucking, commanding D Company, had already had the misfortune to run into them and had been killed. Moreover, difficult to believe but maybe true, was the capture in a farmyard of '15 to 20 English, unconcernedly chopping wood for the breakfast fire, cleaning their weapons and boots, or smoking their pipes'. Referring to our own ambush, the German account tells that when they heard us approaching and heard us stop, it was thought that we had been alerted by the sight of Captain Lucking's vehicle. When we came into view they opened fire with six machine-guns and fifty rifles. In a few seconds it was all over.

Several of us were officially reported killed, myself included. When the letter arrived from the Regimental Office, my sister's grief was mixed with remorse. As she sat on the stairs in tears, she recalled that sometimes she had wished me dead. She was 17 years older than me. She often had to look after me when I was a small boy. I had been an embarrassment to her in her courting days whenever I needed changing. Later on, after my mother became an invalid, she took over the management of the household. She had to see that I got off to school in time, often having to find my cap for me. She also laundered my rugby clothes, usually all muddy. I had been the bane of her life. I was to become even more indebted to her, for she was by far the most regular of my correspondents while I was a POW, writing no fewer than 184 letters.

My father had, before the war, taken out a life insurance

6

No. *Ches/Cas.*

(If replying, please quote above No.)

Army Form B. 104—82B.

15. 6. 19 *40.*

Sir.

It is my painful duty to inform you that a report has been received from the War Office notifying the death of :—

(No.) *4128051*   (Rank) *Pte.*

(Name) *BRICK Samuel Keith Painter*

(Regiment)   CHESHIRE REGT.

which occurred *between 21st & 30th May 1940*

The report is to the effect that he *was killed in action.*

I am to express the sympathy and regret of the Army Council at the soldier's death in his Country's service.

I am,

Sir.

Your obedient Servant,

Eastham Captain

for Officer in Charge of Records.

[76030] 30252/— 500m 9/39 M&C Ltd. **706** Forms/B.104—82B/6   [P.T.O.

policy for me, which he now cashed but happily paid back on receiving news that I was a prisoner. It came over the German radio, in a broadcast by Lord Haw Haw. The dustman happened to have heard it and came rushing to tell my father. The news was subsequently confirmed by the International Red Cross.

I had envisaged being killed or, what seemed worse, badly wounded but not being taken prisoner. That was a let-down. Forced continually to retreat, day and night, hopelessly exposed to attacks from the air, we felt not so much shamed as duped. The German Stukas, dive-bombers fitted with sirens to produce a high-pitched screech, were designed to terrify – and so they did. They had me trying to burrow into the earth with my bare hands. There were only a few Bren guns for our protection and these were totally inadequate.

Nobody had expected the Allied armies to be so decisively overwhelmed. Most of us, I think, had swallowed our own propaganda. We had been led to believe that the German Army was poorly equipped, the German economy overstretched and that we, Britain and France, had finally called Hitler's bluff. But our declaration of war had merely upgraded the phoney peace of 1936–39, when it was hoped that Hitler could be appeased, into a phoney war which, hopefully, would convince Hitler that he had gone too far. It was little better than a charade on our part. Meanwhile, Hitler, safe from attack, prepared the offensive which was to prove so devastating.

The Anglo-French alliance not only failed to deter Hitler; it also became another of his many victims. The Germans, after thrusting unexpectedly through the Ardennes, raced for the Channel ports, splitting the Allied armies asunder and also the alliance. Unable to stave off a crippling defeat, the British and French governments went their separate ways. Britain salvaged what it could of the BEF and kept most of the RAF in reserve for its own defence. France, for its part, was torn between two contrary conceptions of the national interest; on the one hand, Pétain's submission to a fait accompli, and on the other, de Gaulle's defiant continuation of the struggle from overseas.

The fall of France aroused a great deal of mutual recrimination, most of it shown by historians to be ill-founded.[1] It was an Allied defeat rather than something singularly French. France appeared to have been most at fault. Had not France been fielding much the larger land force – 115 divisions, 91 of them facing Germany – whereas the BEF consisted of a mere 10? And had not French generals been entrusted with overall command? That was undeniable; it was none the less an Allied decision. More controversial and partisan was the accusation that the Allies had been defeated because the French had lacked the will to fight. On this point the historians are much more circumspect. We who had been taken prisoner were apt to judge these matters by appearances. Most British POWs had little more than their battledress, whereas quite a number of French POWs were seen to be in possession of all their personal kit, which suggested that they had surrendered without a fight. The contrast was over-drawn and the assumption unwarranted but, in the heat of the moment, this is how appearances were interpreted. In seeking a scapegoat, we made no allowances for the fact that whether one fought or surrendered depended upon the particular circumstances and on the orders given. Large numbers of French troops had found themselves outmanoeuvred and virtually *hors de combat*. It was probably more out of a sense of disgust than of defeatism that most of them lay down their arms. For the BEF it was different. There was some hope of evacuation by sea and it was necessary to fight to the last in order to make that evacuation possible.

[1] This is argued by Martin Alexander in *Decisive Campaigns of the Second World War*, edited by John Gooch, Frank Cass, 1990.

2

Survival: Physical and Mental

Our captors were jubilant. It showed in their faces as they gleefully drove away our trucks and in their voices telling us, in English, 'For you the war is over', a statement which all British POWs seem to have heard. We also heard them singing *'wir fahren gegen England'*. The invasion of England was their next step.

We were soon made aware that the Germans would lose no opportunity to play upon the rift between their British and French prisoners. Harold Marshall and I had been taken to a field hospital but our wounds were fortunately superficial and, after having been examined, we were led away to join some other POWs. These, except for a solitary Irishman, were all French. Whenever there was a job to be done, the Germans would pick on the three British prisoners. A guard would call out *'Wo sind die drei Engländer?'* Some dead horses, much the worse for having lain in that state for several days of exceptionally hot weather, had to be buried. Much worse was the task of clearing up part of the building which had served as a latrine. The pile of excrement had to be shovelled out of the window and the drain cleared with our bare hands. *'Die drei Engländer'*, angered by the fact that none of the French were asked to give a hand, were glad when moved out to join some other British POWs.

More humiliation was to come when we were marched through the streets of Aachen prior to being loaded into cattle trucks. Were we being unnecessarily and deliberately paraded so that the local population could enjoy the spectacle? So it seemed. Neither Harold nor I remember very much of the journey across Germany to Poland. He was weak from loss of blood. I was laid low by fever. We had all been vaccinated and I must have been allergic to whatever it was. Each truck was marked '8 horses or 40 men'. I suspect we were many more than 40. We travelled thus, short of water, food and even air, for the days were still very hot and there was little ventilation. We had no idea of our destination; and while there were many stops, it was only very occasionally that the doors were opened. I discovered, when consulting Harold about it over 50 years later, that we had similar but quite contradictory impressions – I, that he had cared for me throughout the journey; he, that I had taken care of him. We must have taken turns.

In due course, we learnt later how others had fared. Those who had been taken prisoner at a later date, at the time of the withdrawal to Dunkirk told us of 'the march'. The German Army, confronted with such a large number of prisoners, moved them back into Germany on foot. Already exhausted by the fighting, they had to endure this long march, in the heat of the day, suffering hunger and thirst, for they were given very little to eat and their guards invariably prevented them drinking from the pails of water which civilians, taking pity, had placed at the roadside. It was not as long nor so killing as the march inflicted on us towards the end of the war in 1945, in the depth of winter, but it was certainly an ordeal. Harold and I were thankful not to have experienced it.

Our destination turned out to be a town in what had been the Polish Corridor, the strip of territory which had given Poland access to the Baltic but which had separated East Prussia from the rest of Germany. The town had been called Torun when it was part of Poland but had been renamed Thorn by the Germans. We were put in one of the old disused forts built by the Germans in the nineteenth century. This was Fort 13. It lay below ground level, surrounded by a dry moat. It was dank, cavernous and uninviting.[1] We were issued with an identity tag, made of light metal. It was rectangular in shape and perforated along the middle. The number of one's Stalag and one's individual number, in my case Stalag XXA and 5580, was stamped on each of the two sections. In case of death, one half was detached, the other half left on the body. These tags had another, more vital, use. They enabled us to divide a *Kommisbrot*, the standard straight-sided loaf which was our staple diet, into exactly equal portions. It kept the peace on countless occasions.

Every one of those early days was bleak. Morale was low. There was no news from home. We felt isolated. Although we had witnessed at first hand the prowess of the German Army, we found it hard to believe what we were told, namely that France was out of the war [there was no mention of de Gaulle] and that it was Britain's turn to choose between negotiating an armistice or courting an invasion. We had very little to eat – our daily ration was usually a bowl of watery soup, a small portion of bread and either a little margarine or sausage. A sorry spectacle was that of starving men fighting over the empty tubs of soup, for there always remained a few spoonfuls which could be scraped out, if only one could reach them. It never seemed to me worth the effort, never mind the self-contempt it entailed. For clothes, we had to make do with those we were wearing when captured, supplemented by bits of Polish uniform. Clogs replaced worn-out boots. We became infested with lice. Our clothes were occasionally 'deloused' – that is, steamed – and our heads were shaved but the lice soon reappeared. We spent hours every day picking them out of the seams of our clothes and pubic hair and then cracking them between our thumbnails. We also noticed signs of beriberi, a consequence of malnutrition.

My first three cards home are stark reminders of what

[1] In February 1941 some New Zealand officers were sent to one of the forts as a reprisal for alleged ill-treatment of German POWs in Canada. The *Official History of New Zealand in the Second World War* comments that 'the conditions at Thorn could not be reconciled with the spirit of the Geneva Convention'.

preoccupied my mind in that first week of June 1940. Each card had only seven lines, just enough for about seventy words, and virtually all the space is taken up with requests, first for food and secondly for news of what had happened to my friends.

4.6.1940: Postcard

Hello home sweet home – you are far away now. I got a bullet in my left leg but it is OK. Don't send clothes, only food, much chocolate, biscuits, bunloaf, light cake, 'Skippers', oxo, bovril, dates, potted meat and salmon – a weekly parcel of the underlined. Will send a cheque to cover the expense. I am with Harold Marshall. Get in touch with his people.

4.6.1940: Postcard

Don't send any letter with parcels – separately. Please enquire . . . as to George Shaw, Roy Mace and Ian Neil – send me any news of the Batt's welfare. Let my friends know that I am safe. Don't forget to send plenty of chocolate – a few 6d novels – soap . . . I had a few lovely presents for the kids captured – now stitchless.

9.6.1940: Postcard

I can send two letters and four postcards a month. Don't send tinned goods or chemicals or soap in parcels. Send some cooked meat, cheese, jam, any interesting newspaper cuttings. Please write as often as possible and give the address to my friends.

The food requested was an odd assortment, more a list of what I had enjoyed at home rather than what was likely to be most suitable in my new and totally unfamiliar circumstances. The bunloaf would have stood me in good stead: it was an excellent fruit cake which my sister made. My offer to send a cheque may also seem a little odd. It so happened that I had my chequebook on me when captured. I was used to paying something towards my own upkeep. My father had informed me, when I was 16, that he could no longer afford to keep me at school. He had been Mayor of Wallasey the previous year, an honour which had proved expensive. The family business was not always on an even keel. Founded by my grandfather, a shoemaker, in the 1860s, it had grown into a small firm retailing and repairing boots and shoes. It had a good reputation and my father was a good employer, reluctant to lay anybody off even in hard times. I found a job with ICI, at £50 a year. Half of this I handed over to my sister, who ran the household. It was only natural that I would help pay for whatever they now sent me. As for news of my friends, it obviously did not occur to me that our families were no better informed than ourselves. In that first week of June, I was acting like a man in distress. I sent out an SOS – send me food and news – and only later was I able to make a more realistic assessment of my situation. Throughout June I continued to write in much the same vein, confident apparently that I could and would be sustained by 'a weekly parcel', for which I would 'square up later'.

15.6.1940: Letter

This letter can only be a list of requests – once again for food, especially chocolate. Don't forget a parcel a week. Also send a pair of braces, saccharine tablets, three pairs of boot laces, a cheap fountain pen (1/-), a cheap wristlet watch (2/6). I have decided to give up smoking, so don't send tobacco; but if tobacco can be sent free of duty, as to the B.E.F. send 8 oz a month. Forward any interesting mail and interesting bits of the *Wallasey News*. Let all friends know my address but please explain all regulations re *Kriegsgefangenenpost* and restrictions on parcel contents. Let records department of ICI know of me. Explain to all that I cannot write to them. Don't forget to find out the fate of George Shaw, Roy Mace, Ian Neil, Arthur Hoggett, Tom Johnson, Percy McCormick.[1]

Now for news. I am in a prison camp, quite alive and kicking. We do some work; in autumn, I hope, on the land. We get a little pay which we spend at the canteen on bread, toothpaste and necessaries. Send a pack of cards (afterthought). I was taken prisoner in Belgium on May 19 after five days in action. All 5 platoon was destroyed (my platoon). Note my new number. Hope to be home for my 21st.

15.6.1940: Postcard

On all correspondence put 'Prisoner of War' not *Kriegsgefangenpost*: this will ensure free postage... Please write often and the weekly parcel is important. I cannot send a cheque. So note the expense (it will be much) and I will square up later.

22.6.1940: Postcard

... Send a German grammar; there's one in my bedroom – and some Mersey razor blades... Don't forget the weekly parcel. Please keep all my correspondence.

Over the next few weeks, more and more POWs arrived in Torun. The news which they brought of what had been happening in France was not at all reassuring. Harold and I were of course on the lookout for survivors of our battalion and of A Company in particular. We met only one and the

[1] Four of them had been killed.

information he brought could not have been worse. He told us that he had seen Norman Marshall, Harold's younger brother, hit by mortar fire and certainly killed. He had in fact survived his wounds and been taken prisoner. Thus for a time, each brother thought the other to be dead.

The two letters posted in July from Fort 13 show me both saddened and disheartened by the course of events.

30.6.1940: Letter

Almost July; after a spell of glorious sun it now rains. It is six months since I saw home; may I soon be back to the old life. But it will not be the same – there are so many of the lads gone. Today for the first time I realized what it will mean, for Harold learnt that his brother Norman was killed. He was greatly affected. There must be widespread suffering; you must be very thankful that I am alive. I am here, quite safe, until peace. I hear we lost Captain White and Bob Shields.[1] The whole Batt. was involved. My name is in the hands of the Red Cross, but still send a weekly parcel. I am anticipating my first soon. How is Ethel?[2] Do you think that I will be present for the event?... I am told that ICI Billingham has been bombed. I have been doing a little clerking but not permanently. I work for 6 pfennigs an hour – 1 penny an hour, taking twelve RMks to the pound... In parcels send any nutritious concentrates or preserves; also your bunloaf, Nancy.

19.7.1940: Letter

I believe the mail, in both directions, has been suspended for some weeks. I read this in 'Camp', an English

---

[1] My company commander and sergeant major. Captain White was in fact taken prisoner.
[2] My sister-in-law, who was expecting a child in November.

paper[1] which was inaugurated on July 7th The reason given was that the existing facilities were rendered inoperative. Some letters have arrived at the camp; I hope I may receive one before the suspension commenced. Some St John Ambulance parcels arrived, twelve to a parcel. I got a tin of beef stew; Toss[2] a packet of tea. There are strong rumours that you can send a parcel only once every three months, and then only chocolate. I hope this is not the case, because I am relying so on them. 'Camp' tells us that France has signed a peace pact and gives the terms: that we lost 792 planes since June 4th (before that we had lost about 3,000) that we have lost 492,000 tons of shipping since the middle of May. I wish Wallasey could have such a summer as we are having here – but then in winter it is about 40 degrees below. On Sunday a German general is visiting the Fort. Last Sunday we had a service, when we all thought of homes and families. Germany wants peace, so do I. May I see you soon – how soon?

Peace, an honourable peace, with a Germany which had triumphed in France, in time to get us home for Christmas, was of course a delusion. But if we had not deluded ourselves, survival would have been even more difficult.

My immediate concern was to survive in as good a shape as possible, physically and mentally. I was fortunate in two respects. First, in these very difficult days of 1940, some of us stood a better chance than others simply because we had had a more fortunate upbringing, especially in having been better nourished. I was once in the cemetery at Torun, attending a burial service. I noticed the ages of the POWs buried there. So many were of my age, and I could not help thinking that in all probability starvation had contributed to their deaths. I attributed the fact that I was carrying a wreath, rather

---

[1] A news-sheet in English put out by the Germans for us to read.
[2] Harold Marshall's nickname.

than being carried in the coffin, to all the good food I had eaten in my youth.[1]

Secondly I had a very close companion, Harold Marshall. It was most important to have a 'mate' whom one could trust unreservedly and in whom one could confide. Starvation and dispossession had reduced us to the condition feared by the seventeenth-century philosopher Thomas Hobbes, namely 'a war of all against all'. In this battle for individual survival, no one can feel secure, not even the physically strong, for the weak can think themselves more astute; they are not intimidated from challenging the strong to a battle of wits. There is a story which illustrates the degree of mistrust which prevailed and how necessary, yet how difficult, it was to keep watch over one's few remaining possessions. Someone had a loaf which he was keeping for the morrow. He thought it would be safe if he used it as a pillow. But in the morning he found himself with a loaf shortened at each end. It is a plausible story, and several ex-POWs have vouched for its veracity, but I suspect it was invented, like so many other good stories. I was lucky because I found in Harold a ready-made companion. We had trodden the same path: school, Scouts, tennis club and, for nine months of the war, trained and fought in the same platoon. As POWs we became as close as brothers.

Fortunately, when the time came to be moved out of Fort 13, we left together. Fort 13 was but a transit camp for those on their way to or from an *Arbeitskommando*, that is one of the many labour camps which had been established wherever our labour was in demand – usually factories, building sites, roads and farms. Most of my time as a POW was spent in work camps of one kind or another.

Many of us who were obliged to work, the privates and lance corporals, envied the non-working NCOs locked up in Fort 15, who had time to study, play music, and put on plays.

---

[1] 'Probably 80% of the graves, more than a hundred, in the cemetery of Torun bore the date of the winter of 1940/41.' (David Wild, *Prisoner of Hope*, p. 151.)

Conversely, they thought that we were the lucky ones. A work camp was seen as a place which provided not only better food but also a change of scenery, more freedom, contact with Polish civilians and an opportunity to escape – all psychological advantages which were thought to outweigh the obligation to work.

It is impossible to say, in general, whether it was better to be working or not working. Too much of the one was probably as bad as too much of the other. Probably most would have welcomed a change from time to time, even if it might have meant jumping out of the frying pan into the fire. Either way, nearly five years was much too long. Also, so much depended upon the individual, his range of interests, his abilities, his particular strengths and weaknesses. I can only speak for myself and of my own reactions to life on an *Arbeitskommando*. I was often out of tune with the others.

Not all work camps were the same and some were distinctly better than others. However, with few exceptions, there was no escaping the Polish winter. It was no joy to be working out of doors in temperatures well below zero, especially if there was a wind. All day long we felt frozen. We rarely had gloves. On one occasion, when lifting some girders, my hands were stuck to the metal. In nearly all camps the work left us exhausted and all we wanted to do was to climb into bed. Only on Sundays did we have time and energy to wash clothes, write a letter and read a book. Only a few work camps corresponded to what was generally considered to be the ideal – a camp of not more than 20 men working in ones and twos on small farms, and only one guard who could not keep an eye on everybody at the same time.

Our first work camp was quite large, more than a hundred of us. It was situated near Gydnia, renamed Gotenhafen by the Germans. It took us out of the jurisdiction of Stalag XXA into that of Stalag XXB, and close to the Baltic sea. In theory, we should all have been planning an escape to Sweden, on one of the Swedish boats sailing from Danzig or Gotenhafen. Although we were there for a whole year, neither Harold nor I seriously contemplated escape, nor, as far as I'm aware, did any of the others. Escape was not lightly undertaken. Not because it was forbidden and heavily punished. The Geneva Convention recognises that a POW has a duty to make the attempt. We were restrained much more by the improbability of making a successful escape and perhaps, in those early days, by the delusion that the war might soon be over. In any case, one had to weigh the chances of success against the consequences for others. After an escape, the Germans invariably clamped down, carried out searches and made life more unpleasant than usual. Those who attempted to escape were not always the most popular. It was only in 1943 that I was given a chance to make an escape with some chance of success. While at Gotenhafen, despite the proximity of shipping, escape was not a question which agitated my mind. I was preoccupied with getting through each day's fatigue. Is that the meaning of 'sufficient unto the day is the evil thereof'?

Food and news continued to be the major preoccupation. There was some improvement of the one but not of the other. Our daily rations were much better than they had been in Fort 13 and Red Cross parcels began to arrive. There were also opportunities, when out working, provided the guards were not too vigilant, to slip away just long enough to contact one of the Polish civilian workers. They unstintingly gave us their sandwiches. It was also possible to trade. I was one of the last to sacrifice a watch. I was reluctant to let it go for just two or three loaves. But having become the only one with a watch, able to tell how much time remained before we knocked off work, I preferred the bread to being continually pestered for the time.

We were put to work building a road and then digging trenches for the laying of pipes. The worksite was not always close at hand and the march to and from work added to both the length of the working day and the fatigue. Winter, when we were marched to work before sunrise, was the hardest time. We worked so slowly digging the trenches – hidden from the guards by their very depth – that we were put on piece work. This suited us better. It kept us warmer and got us back to camp quicker. Another of our jobs, the laying of a path along the seashore at Zoppot, involved collecting pebbles all day. The sea itself was frozen.

The move to Gotenhafen was an improvement on Fort 13, except for an interruption to the mail for some unknown reason. Incoming mail was scanty and we were allowed to write, in the whole final three months of the year, just one letter and seven cards.

7.9.1940: Postcard

I haven't been able to write for some time. I have just received two letters ... that is 4 I have had to date. I have shared in one Red Cross parcel; how surprising to taste again marmalade and cheese. Send all the clothes and chocolate you can. I'm keeping well, hope you are all safe. Write often and regular; mail is next to food.

14.9.1940: Letter

Regular writing on my part resumed, so expect the usual quota ... I will consider myself lucky if I see it[1] through without illness; so far only cuts and a sore throat. Although I still have a cheque book I have no other kit. You ought to see my socks. We have a special paper, the 'Camp' which gives the news, foreign and home. It says Liverpool docks have been bombed, that there's a $16\frac{2}{3}\%$ levy on boots and shoes. Bad for business. The present camp is much better than I expected; also prison life. Reveille 4:30 a.m.; parade for work 5:45 a.m.; back from work at 4 p.m. when we have a bowl of stew. Rations for the day are $\frac{1}{2}$ a brown loaf and some margarine and sausage. We can also buy $\frac{1}{2}$ a white loaf from the

[1] The coming winter.

22

canteen. We are road-building now. I am learning German; try and send a grammar. If possible also Shakespeare's plays, an anthology of verse and a book on economics. I hope you have seen the Marshalls; he and I are still together; of the others I know nothing ... send some photographs.

22.9.1940: Postcard

B's birthday: many happy returns. Mine next Sunday. Let's hope it is the only one in prison. Letters reach us in batches after two months' transit: some don't get through, however; it is just a question of luck. Have received acknowledgement of subscription to Cheshire branch of Red Cross. Have only heard from you: no others. We are told Liverpool has been heavily bombed. Good luck. Still OK.

Xmas Day 1940 – the first of five as a POW – was spent trying to be jovial. I wrote a mournful card home that day.

25.12.1940: Postcard

Today we had $1\frac{1}{2}$ loaves and some fish – like the biblical feast, but we left no crumbs. An English speaking padre gave a service. We also had 2 bottles of beer – no smokes. Xmas Eve, an improvised band and a dance, minus the girls, entertained us and the guards. Xmas Day a little sad thinking of you all. I suppose everyone really wants peace. No Red Cross. No mail. It's a life of hopes.

But ten days later I was able to write in a much more cheerful mood.

5.1.1941: Letter

A letter at last. It's new year, happy and prosperous. Red Cross parcels have arrived, sufficient for 2 a man. A parcel to myself has been my ambition since May but I had lost hope. After occasional minute portions a whole parcel is such a windfall that we are like children. To renew the tastes of tinned fruit, syrup, cocoa, tea, chocolate etc. was as exciting as the first letter... May you all be safe; I am out of this war and my turn to worry for your safety. I regret missing leave[1]... Toss and I have a new friend, Williams of Cardiff. Here real friendship is invaluable but very limited. I realise now what a hell Army life would have been outside 'A' Coy. I wish we were still together. Toss and I have been indispensable to one another, sharing joy and sorrow. We welcome Les, who is new blood. This life is very exhausting and nerve-racking, and interests are so few that friendship, real friendship, is the only safeguard against madness or depression. Somehow we three are always talking, a good antidote. Climate is severe – perpetual snow. Send more clothes and soap. How's John and his elephants?[2]

Harold Marshall, Les Williams and I kept one another company virtually the whole of 1941. Our apparently inexhaustible conversation often led to us being asked, 'What do you talk about?' Williams was a good talker, and, as we were to discover, a spinner of tales. We were led to believe that he was well educated, and that he came from a prosperous family in Cardiff, his father being head of a company manufacturing soft drinks. Spinning tales was a common pastime among POWs but usually implausibilities and inconsistencies in what one was being told suspended belief. Williams fooled us

[1] UK leave for the BEF had started in April.
[2] My brother, who was with the Nigerian regiment.

24

completely. It did not matter, he had helped to relieve our boredom. Had we met again after the war, no doubt we would have had a good laugh, but it was not to be. He died of tuberculosis while still a POW. When we made contact with his family after the war, we realised the extent to which he had been pulling our leg.

We stayed in Gotenhafen for a whole year, from July 1940 to the beginning of August 1941 – long enough to enable my family to gain, from my letters, some idea of how my days were spent and what I thought of it all. Of course, there were incidents which could not be mentioned. One day, an officer, visiting the camp, fell into a rage on seeing who was our *Vertrauensmann* (the person who acted as intermediary between us and the camp commandant, translating to us the commandant's orders and to him our requests). This happened to be Sergeant Fred Mulley, who after the war served in a Labour government as Minister of Defence. His offence was to be a Jew. Fortunately, Mulley suffered no more than verbal abuse, and his dismissal as our *Vertrauensmann*.

10.2.1941: Letter

Ack. letters... Also 2nd clothing parcel containing pyjamas, pumps etc. I eagerly await chocolate. Am OK for clothes now, except socks, handkerchiefs. Send regularly soap and toothpaste. The months are passing – winter will soon be out, after the coming winds. It hasn't been as rigorous as I expected, although there has been continual snow and ice for months. Working in it has been unpleasant, but France was a good rehearsal. Lately, I have been working in the woods, supplying fuel for the camp fires. Each room has a stove. The only complaint I have is that we are overcrowded, but that may be remedied. Nancy seems very worried about my bed. We were on the floor but now we have 3-tier bunks and straw palliasses. Better than France... If any people wish to send me anything, tell them books. Send Penguins 261, 283, 243, 237.

Pelican A12, A3, A4, A17, A52. I am dipping into psychology. *NW Passage.* Some of the lads went through worse than that before reaching the camp, but being wounded Toss and I were lucky.

16.3.1941: Letter

I have just attempted to make pancakes. My mixture was too thin. There's an orgy of eating, forgetful of the morrow. Toss, Les and I are in a road-making party, still smiling. The sun is showing itself, thank God... This day last year we were going up for a 3 weeks' stretch in front of the Maginot line. A thrilling experience. There is a scheme for POWs to continue studies. I have made enquiries. We have had 27 Gold Flake [cigarettes] each. Please send cigarettes. I am smoking again... I will be a proper labourer by the time I finish this – never be without a means of livelihood. The 'Camp' tells us of our African successes, but these are checked by German reinforcements. Plenty of shipping losses. What will spring bring? The young Germans are very confident. Personally I think it will be a long war. I didn't have enough of it not to wish to be in it again. It's the air force that counts. Remember how I wanted to transfer. Just my luck.

27.4.1941: Letter

Recd. no mail for a fortnight... Universal rationing of bread introduced; our ration reduced from 800 to 450 grams. And Red Cross parcels a dim memory. Toss's Jan. parcel with 3 lbs chocolate an opportune 'corn in Egypt'. Socks, soap, toothpaste send regularly – above that just chocolate. Would you like to write to Les's people? The Marshalls are no doubt already in touch. It's Sunday afternoon; nearly everybody deservedly sleeps. It's peaceful and restful; but I ache for a break in the monotony of waiting, of labouring, of this imposed denial of luxuries. I am tired of the same faces; they are not good company, excepting Toss and Les. We three try to amuse each other. I am glad my army life was eased by so many of the Wallasey lads... Reading is the only solace but book parcels seem to have ceased. Also the cigarette parcels. I had hoped to spend my 21st at home. Alas, no girls, no champagne, no dance. I'll have a party when I return, but I'm out of touch with the girls. I'd like to go to sleep for the duration...

11.5.1941: Letter

Toss is writing this for me as I slightly cut my finger opening a Xmas pudding – a worthy cause... Glad to hear we escaped damage in the March raid. I feel much easier now that you are sleeping at Heswall...[1] 100 men are leaving the camp but I do not think we are included. We are settled down here and rather reluctant to move, although it would break the monotony. This May we have had 3 snowfalls, not quite English spring weather. Don't forget chocolate is predominant article in parcels. This morning the band (violin, banjolele [*sic*], mandolin) gave a short entertainment in the sun. Two parcels containing plenty of chocolate arrived for Les today. The sun, the music and the chocolate made this Sunday one worthy to see out the first year of *Gefangenschaft*. How many years to go. Please see about sending cigarettes and tobacco... When we have Red Cross parcels we are quite happy, without them it is punishment.

---

[1] In the Wirral, some miles from the docks of Merseyside.

22.6.1941: Letter

We have received 3 more Red Cross food parcels and 100
fags. That's a total of 13 and 200 respectively... I hope
John[1] is having a better, and less depressing, fight than I
had. It's no fun retreating each day. Perhaps he is reveng-
ing me. Today is a very quiet Sunday, lovely and peaceful, a perfect sun shining... It's strange to think that this
won't reach you for another two months, for such a lot
can happen by then... I'm a deep brown now, for we
work minus shirts. Hope there's no need for me to labour
when I return, for I don't like it. In winter, it's cruel, and
I'm hoping I may not have to stamp my feet and slap my
body again...

When I wrote 'for such a lot can happen by then', I was
probably making a veiled reference to the news that Germany
had just launched its attack on the Soviet Union. The news that
Germany had one more enemy was good news. Our appetite
for good news could sometimes be greater than our appetite
for food. Now that Red Cross parcels were arriving with some
regularity, we could to some extent satisfy both. There were
items in the food parcels which we could trade, either with a
guard or with one of the civilians. The prime items for trading
were coffee and chocolate, both of which had virtually disappeared from the shops. A cup of real coffee was as much a
treat to the Germans as was a cup of tea to us. Provided there
was someone in the camp who knew how to assemble and
work a radio, it was worth trying to trade for all the necessary
bits and pieces.

I do not know whether, at Gotenhafen, anyone had access to
a radio. The need for secrecy was obviously of paramount
importance and only very few would have known. It was only
after the war was over that those who had been involved in
such activities could reveal the ingenious ways radios had

[1] My brother.

been hidden. The searches which the guards carried out from time to time could be quite thorough but only rarely was a radio discovered. But even without a radio it was possible, especially for those of us who worked outside the camp, to pick up much more of the news than was to be gained by reading *Camp*. The Poles would pass on to us whatever they knew. Because reliable news was often so scarce, we fed on rumour. I developed a strong antipathy to rumour. It was usually so wild as to be incredible. I preferred, whenever I had access to a German newspaper such as the *Volkischer Beobachter*, to read between the lines. When the war turned against Germany, one could learn a lot that way.

Later that summer, the camp at Gotenhafen was closed down and we were sent to work on farms. We were not sure that this was going to be a change for the better; probably not, for we had begun to settle down to quite a well-organised state of existence.

13.7.1941: Postcard

Prosperity: 4 more Red Cross parcels and 100 fags received. This past week a scorcher. Too hot in the sun: about 86 Fahrenheit. Brown as a berry. Felt quite at home today – sunbathing on the grass outside, having had early morning tea and porridge later, the accordion playing merry tunes, everybody in good spirits. Dancing with Les, an expert, to the band in the evening...

2.8.1941: Letter

Monday the camp closes. We are to become farm lab-ourers ... which means anything up to 14 hours a day, and hard work. After this camp it is not going to be agreeable, where we had so many amenities (only last week a gramophone and a dozen English records) and of late such comfortable quarters. It means more food but less leisure. In the camp we have a future supply of Red Cross parcels (until Sept 13): we won't be able to carry all those (7) but last night we were issued one and tomorrow another two. I don't know about the rest. Rather changed circumstances from this time last year, when we were minus parcels, letters and clothing. It has been a long journey since then but after the privations of last summer and the rigours of the winter were forgotten, it has been rather pleasant. These adjectives are only comparative. But I suppose we can take it. Carrying the kit is the problem, without valises. I shall want a year's holiday after this. Not knowing conditions in England I cannot picture my future at all. All I know is that I'm going farming now... A lot of rain just lately but we don't mind that – it stops work here.

A few days after writing that letter I was bringing in the harvest – and back-breaking work it was, both for horses and men. Very little of the work was mechanised. The corn was cut with a horse-drawn reaper, but bound by hand into sheaves, stacked and later loaded on to horse-drawn carts with a pitchfork. Threshing was a non-stop affair. As soon as one cart has been unloaded into the thresher, another arrived. There was no escaping the noise of the machine and the dust. The only way to have a break was to choose the heaviest job, that of waiting for the sacks to fill. They had to be weighed, slung over one's shoulders, carried up a ladder, and tipped out onto the upper floor of the barn. Each sack weighed about 70 kilos.

17.8.1941: Letter

...Now farming... It's a party of 10, but we are split up into different farms ... we 3 are together still on quite a large farm. We were lucky, because they feed us very well, but we must work hard. We have surprised ourselves working. While the sun is in the sky we work, and we finish work only to wash and get thankfully into bed. Sunday is free, and today we went swimming. For sleeping, the 10 of us use a central billet. This is the sort of life that either makes or breaks you. Fortunately, I seem to have taken to this farming, binding, staking sheaves, threshing. Quite at home with the pitch fork. I have used horse and machine, but not yet the scythe or the plough. Wheat, oats, rye and barley, sugar beet and potatoes we grow. Although it's very hard work, that fact, together with the good food and plenty of milk, will be better for me than some of the terrible conditions of the previous year. No time for reading now but this may only be for a couple of months. I'd like to stay the winter, however...

31.8.1941: Letter

You'd better polish up your agricultural vocabulary for all my letters will be full of news from the farm. We're in the midst of threshing, and do I know it. My farm, Klassen's, is one of the largest round here, about 15 acres, and is by far the most proficient and well-organised. In fact, his threshing is a perfect example of organisation. It's 100% efficiency from machine and men and horses. There's the father, son and grandson. The father is semi-retired, a jovial gentleman. The son is a cavalry officer on leave for the harvest: he is a taskmaster of violent temper, but the brains of the organisation. Fortunately, he thinks I'm a good worker, which is what counts. The grandson is one of those detestable little brats of 5, who ought to be packed off to school. Both wives are very nice. What German I knew proved very useful here and it's rapidly improving. It's much more varied and interesting work than in the old camp, and of course we work in the fields without continual supervision of a guard. Toss has been moved onto another farm but I see him at nights. I now weigh 142 lbs, against 168 stripped April '40. That's 2 stone lost, but I feel none the

31

worse. It's incredible that I'm only 10 stone and that I carry sacks of 150 lbs upstairs and everywhere...

Later in the autumn we moved to another farm, where the work, harvesting the sugar beet, was even more exhausting. It was all done by hand like everything else. We used a two-pronged fork, about 30 to 40 centimetres in length. It had, low down, a foot-rest used to press the fork down into the hard sun-baked earth. Then the long tapering sugar beet was prised out of the earth by pulling with one hand and levering with the other. It was back-breaking work. Moreover, we worked in a line and had to keep up with a *Vorarbeiter*, the lead man, a peasant used to such work, who had the pick of the forks. The field of beet stretched out of sight and the guard appeared from time to time to see that one did not fall far behind the others. That was how I spent my twenty-first birthday. I had sent a card home the previous day.

28.9.1941: Postcard

My last day of youth. I'm getting old. I'll spend tomorrow among the sugar-beet. How I love it. I challenge anyone I know to come straight from what he is doing and do just one hour's sugar-beet. He'll wonder what happened to his back, his right shoulder and wrists. It lasts for weeks. I'd like a holiday stoking. What a 21st.

Luck was with me that autumn. I had a brush with one of the guards which might easily have had serious consequences. It was a Sunday, the one free day of the week, and the three of us had slipped out. We wanted to call on some Polish workers who were housed not very far away. We were on our way back when I realised I had left my jacket behind. I retrieved it but by then a search for us had been started. The guard who had already apprehended my companions was waiting for me on the road. He had no love for us, having lost a brother in France in 1940. He flew into a rage and laid into me. I was lucky. I might easily have shared the fate of the POW on a neighbouring farm. I saw the body soon after the shooting. He had obviously been shot at very close range, half his head having been blasted away. It is a sight which still haunts me.

5.10.1941: Letter

...Well I am now a man, according to law. I spent my 21st amongst the sugar-beet – one of the hardest day's work of my life. But they say hard work killed no man. Fortunately, the weather is wonderful. I still work without a shirt in the early afternoon. It's bad when wet and cold. Actually we're lucky being on farms, because of the decent food. Two hot dinners a day is a considerable advantage even if it is only potatoes[1]... I had a good feed of chocolate on my 21st, for the monthly supply of Red Cross parcels arrived that day and we had one good feed. I also fried bacon and sausages. I'm still 145 lbs but as well as can be. This work doesn't give me much chance to be browned off: it keeps me fit and helps my German...

At the end of the month (October 1941), the harvest finished, we were returned to Stalag XXB's transit camp at Marienwerder (Kwidzyn). We prayed we would not be sent to a sugar-beet factory. These operated for a relatively short period, starting in late autumn, and by all accounts, conditions were unpleasant. We wondered what else might be in store for us. The essential was to stick together, Harold, Les and I. After a fortnight's uncertainty, we were dispatched to near Elbing, a town just inside East Prussia. We found ourselves once again part of a fairly large-sized group, as in Gotenhafen, to work in a variety of ways.

---

[1] I calculated that I ate 25 lb of them a week.

One very welcome indoor job came my way – removing the blackout paint from some windows. They were almost at roof height, in a tall building. The sun, shining through the glass, kept me warm, and perched at that height I was not bothered by any guard checking my work. I had been given a tin of solvent to use. All went well, until it was discovered that I had used as much solvent on one short stretch of windows as should have sufficed for the whole job. I had been happy saving my own energy by using up the Reich's scarce resources.

28.12.1941: Letter

Another Xmas over... I had three days off, worked yesterday, and today, being Sunday, again free. A welcome holiday. Our rations were unaltered but fortunately we had a parcel Xmas Eve, complete with pudding, cake, biscuits, chocolate. I had given up hope of having a white Xmas, but no – Xmas Eve brought about 4" and now it is quite thick – and cold. That night we had a fancy dress ball, I was a judge, Toss an ancient Briton. There were some really clever efforts, especially as girls, and 'a good time was had by all'. Sing-song carried on well into the morning. We had a concert next day. Booze would have helped the party along, but the best we could do was a sniff of Chivers Xmas pudding. I've eaten five so far, and have another to come. I've played quite a bit of Monopoly over the holidays... Keep the baccy supply up – it's very valuable now...

15.2.1942: Letter

Ack. 120 cigarettes from ICI... Your letters seem to be coming through very much delayed – from 6 weeks to 2 months in transit... The other day was winter at its worst, a raging blizzard which piled up drifts of 4 to 5 feet all over the place. Fortunately, I was inside that day. But now the sun is quite warm – the duck boards show beneath the ice, and water pours in small torrents off the roofs. I suppose it would be a sensation for a horse and sleigh to glide swiftly down Liscard Rd [Wallasey], bell clanging merrily, but here they almost form traffic blocks. The sky is a lovely blue and the sun shines even when there's a cutting wind making you cover all except your eyes... It's not as good as my previous camp for even now we work from 7 am–5:30 pm but still we are warm, feeding well on Red Cross, and have continuous hot water to wash. It's just a question of taking the rough with the smooth, not making it too rough for oneself, and waiting patiently. We all await the spring but we aren't the most anxious.[1]

3.3.1942: Letter

... There's a spell of thaw this week. This means slush at midday and smooth ice early morning... I hope that parcel with the farm boots arrives before the real thaw. Life at the moment is very mundane – work, read, sleep. Reading a bit of Scott at the moment. Waiting for the spring is exacting. I'm very impatient and restless, just like a bud aching to burst. But I want to bloom into a free man, not a farm labourer... Health OK. We three are still smiling, and hoping.

[1] I think this was a reference to the war on the Russian front.

3

Pride Before a Fall

The rest of 1942 brought quite a few changes, mostly for the better. We had been heartened by Russian and American participation in the war, albeit continually frustrated by our own inactivity. Regular supplies of parcels, of food and clothing, had changed our appearance. In several of my letters, I drew comparisons with 1940. We were no longer slaving and lice-ridden, no longer clad in rags and clogs, no longer reduced to a bare existence.

Certain fundamentals had not changed: the feeling of being caged in, even when working on a farm; the regret that as years slipped by, we were being denied the normal opportunities of life, to advance a career by gaining skills and experience, and possibly establish oneself as an eligible young man. Eagerly awaited photographs of family and friends, of marriages and new arrivals, showed me how I was being left behind. I had missed my twenty-first, what else? Those fighting far from home, in Africa, India and Burma, may have felt the same but I doubt whether it could have been quite so intense, so sustained. It became a recurrent theme in my letters home. POWs, however, did have the opportunities, perhaps more than did those still fighting, to prepare for civilian life by studying and sitting examinations. It was a powerful antidote to the tedium of waiting. Having already passed the intermediate examination of the Chartered Institute of Secretaries in 1939, and won second place in the Liverpool area, I was keen to continue. How far I would have that opportunity depended largely on chance: the Germans, not I, decided where I should be put, what I should do.

In the spring of 1942 instead of being moved to a farm as expected, I was transferred to a cheese factory while Harold and Les were sent elsewhere. That was a blow. For nearly two years we had shared everything, told each other everything. Together we had seen through the worst of conditions, now I was on my own for the first time. I cannot recall how the separation occurred nor how we said goodbye to one another, and it so happens that the letters and cards which I wrote home mid-March to mid-June have been lost.

I worked part of the time in the factory, a hot steamy place, and part of the time in the storage cellar where the cheeses were stored, a cold sunless place. The cheeses were delivered from the farms in wooden crates, about ten to a crate, and stored in refrigerated rooms until needed by the factory nearby. The crates had to be stacked one on top of the other, five or six high, all by hand for there were no such things as fork-lifts. The factory made a processed cheese called Tilsiter, and from each batch of cheeses a sample was taken so that the right blend could be achieved. It was part of my job to take the samples, using the kind of instrument used for removing apple cores. I got to know all the best cheeses and took many a sample for my own consumption.

I remained in this working party for the rest of 1942. My letters relayed home a picture of how life had improved, thanks to the parcels we received.

21.6.1942: Letter

...It is Sunday afternoon in the month of June... You must enjoy the open air after being in an air raid shelter. Just so, I love the dazzling sun and blue sky today after spending the week in the storage cellar. Having overcome long ago the inclination for melancholy brooding over

37

what might have been, I can enjoy the pleasures of the moment.

6.7.1942: Letter

Send me if possible more photos of John and his bride... By the time I get home there may be new nephews and nieces. I'm the only one left now. It won't be a 21st but a marriage that I'll have to celebrate when I get back... We have a new tennis table and in the cool of the evening I had a few rounds with the gloves. Parcels have been arriving thick and fast, and mail arriving in three weeks. Continuous supply of Red Cross parcels since April and stocks here sufficient for August. I remember the days of '40 when we had heard of, but rarely seen them; and the thought of one a week – well, our dreams never aspired to such luxury. I'm still not smoking and I might never start again.[1] But continue to send the fag parcels. We are working longer hours now, due to overtime. Usually 11 to 12 hours a day, sometimes more. I'd like to be on the farms again but it could be a lot worse.

16.8.1942: Letter

I've been comparing today and the circumstances of summer 1940. We are not the same people. Then we were dispirited, sick, and dressed in rags, a pitiable spectacle. Now we are the gentlemen of England – perfectly groomed, creased trousers, sparkling boots. I've just been ironing a couple of shirts. And physically how much improved we are – that goes without saying. I weighed myself stripped yesterday – 11 st 2 lbs. This morning

[1] I did.

being Sunday I had my usual 3 rounds with the gloves, something I never could have done in 1940. Today we are fit, smart and respected. Whenever I see the Russians I think of ourselves in those far off days. Why, I have almost forgotten what agony it was to be hungry. I received the 2 photos of John. I envy his liberty and prospects. The most aggravating snag to me is that I am ambitious, and here that is an instrument of self-torture. Everything in my daily life is ordered for me. I've little choice for meals, for work, or for company. I miss Williams and Toss, for we three were enough company to one another. I've as yet found no substitute, except a book and even there the choice is restricted. Still, compared with 1940, I'm happy and prosperous.

28.8.1942: Postcard

... This camp is going sports-mad – we have PT classes now, and we lap the coal-heap a couple of dozen times and then get under the hose pipe to cool off.

4.10.1942: Letter

... Last Friday we had a film show. It's hoped shortly to arrange a talkie. It was amusing to see the silents again. Life is prosperous at the moment. A regular supply of food parcels, extra food parcels from America[1] and private parcels of cigarettes and books. I can remember different days. I've turned off reading a little and that's where I miss Marshall and Williams. Give me news of Marshall please... On my birthday I was de-bagged and decorated. I'm friendly with a good crowd here and we have some rough comedy occasionally. What I miss is

---

[1] These came from Rotary International. I received four in the summer of 1942.

more intellectual company. Try to send some history books out – English history from Elizabeth. It wouldn't comfort me to read earlier for there was a 100 year war. On the other hand there was a 6 weeks' war in 1866. How dear is Blighty to me. I often read Rupert Brooke's The Old Vicarage, Granchester:

God I will pack and take a train
And get to England once again

I wish I could.

1.11.1942: Letter

I've just finished ironing. You would laugh to see me in my chef's hat, glistening white, pleated and looking on top like a warped piece of plywood. Can you imagine me? I've changed over to the factory and now work where the cheese is actually made. It's very hot – about 80 F and over. We just wear overalls and little slippers – clogs, and the white hats. We make a fine impression of cleanliness and smartness, both inside and outside the factory. Not working in uniform we can keep the khaki in good condition, trousers well creased etc and boots well polished. I have my cap badge shining. Working in conditions where we can keep clean and tidy encourages us to be as smart and soldierly as possible. We are everywhere respected, admired and envied. Thanks to the Red Cross and our intrinsic self-respect, we are a very different picture to 1940. Today is our most prosperous period. A parcel regularly every week, private parcels arriving well for me, feeling fit and inured to patient waiting. This week, those wool-lined jack-boots arrived. They are the envy of the camp and a very fine advert for Brick's Boots. They are ideal – and it's like stepping on a thick pile carpet once again. The slacks are also very welcome ...

15.11.1942: Letter

... Health is still excellent. You ask me about studying. If
I were an NCO I would join the non-workers and study
all day. They have a wonderful chance. As it is I have to
work ten hours a day, and a crowded noisy room is no
place for concentration. We are very encouraged by news
of our new landing in Africa and we are confident Jerry
will soon be out of Africa altogether. Rommel is named
as their best general but we are confident and all wish we
were out there making ourselves useful. Tell me about the
utility shoes and utility clothing... By the time you get
this I judge it will be Xmas. May it be the last of the war.
I think that's the wish of the whole world and not just we
POWs. Let me know if you shall sit down to an 18
pounder but don't worry about me. The Red Cross will
see that I celebrate. Merry Xmas and a war-less New
Year.

My subsequent description of how we celebrated Christmas
1942 was so euphoric that a single letter provided insufficient
space. I somehow managed to get hold of an extra one. They
both arrived home the same day, 3 February 1943, and no
doubt caused some raising of eyebrows.

27.12.1942: Letter

Well Xmas is over and I don't seem to have had a
moment's rest... I never realised I was taking on such a
big job when I became 'general director of entertainment', especially when I had only a fortnight to prepare. I
had to bully fourteen men to shift beds and kit, in order to
have one room free and the other crowded by forty men.
In the free room I built a stage worthy of any dramatics
society – perfectly level ... smoothly working curtains ...
and marvel of marvels a spotlight. Secondly, the stage,
two Xmas trees, and both rooms had to be decorated and

41

there was absolutely no coloured paper to be bought anywhere. Thirdly, I had to put on a concert, written, produced and managed by myself, and in addition I had to act several parts. All that was easy compared with asking twenty times a day the firm for wood, nails, electrical equipment, chairs, clothes, musical instruments etc. Fortunately the works manager was helpful and I had a man to run the band (accordion, drums, clarinet, mouth organ, spoons) and an electrician who knew his stuff... Many were warning me about causing so much inconvenience and overcrowding to put on such an elaborate stage, lights and maybe an uninteresting concert.

Well, on Xmas eve we had a very successful dance. The drums, borrowed from the firm, throbbed rhythm into everybody and the spotlight flickered over the dancers. It was a fancy dress ball and, as a prize was offered, we had some good efforts. The winner dressed as a country yokel and he had a wonderfully made model whippet with him [I think he was a Geordie]. I was quite a realistic ATS girl. Individual songs and community singing broke up the dancing, and at midnight no one was absent from an all-round greeting of 'Merry Xmas'. We all sat down together for Xmas dinner and thought of you folks home doing the same. Concert was Xmas night and it was a three and a half hour show, non-stop. It went down fine. I think I was the most surprised. The main sketch – about life at the cheese works – was a great success – also a bar room sketch – and the stage stood up stoutly to an exhibition of highland dancing. The beginning was a bit slow but by the end the audience never missed a laugh. The 'girls' acted very well. Boxing night we had a whist-drive and a go-as-you-please song and dance. Four of us put on a comedy act. I was dressed as a beach girl, complete with blue slacks, brassiere, blonde wig and panama hat. Today, to my regret, we dismantled everything... I shall remember it, for it was my Xmas and feel proud of the success, when 14 days ago everything seemed impossible.

Alas these letters, full of exuberance and conceit, turned out to be a case of pride before a fall. By the time my letters arrived home my circumstances had changed radically. I was on my way to the *Straflager* at Graudenz, a centre for punishing offenders. My offence was twofold. First, I had attempted to steal some of the cheese. The works manager who had helped to make our Christmas party such fun must have had second thoughts about me when I was caught a few days later misappropriating one of his best cheeses. I immediately found myself under arrest. Secondly, I had become friendly with the young lady in the storage cellar who kept the books recording deliveries and dispatches of cheese – too friendly. After my arrest, my kit was searched and a piece of paper found on which she had written the words of a German song which I had wanted to learn.

My knowledge of German stood me in good stead on the day of the trial. It enabled me to check the interpreter's translation of what I had to say in my own defence. At one point, I intervened to make a correction. I had admitted to putting a cheese aside but I had not actually disposed of it. I was hoping to give it to the Russian prisoners who were desperately hungry. Had one passed by, I would have given it to him – but none did. My insistence on the conditional tense – *hätte einer vorbeigegangen* – had probably no influence on the verdict that I was guilty of theft. But it showed my interest in the German language and helped perhaps to convince the court that my interest in German songs was purely literary. The young lady's testimony in court confirmed this. A lot was at stake. I was facing the prospect of six months' to two years' punishment, for that was the usual sentence in such matters. I was sentenced to two months for stealing the cheese and an extra week for the (more excusable?) misdemeanor of apparently quite innocent fraternisation.

A few weeks elapsed between my trial in mid-January and the start of my sentence in early March. These were spent with other POWs who like myself had offended in some way or another and awaited their punishment. We constituted what was known as '*S*' *Kommando*. I anticipated that once in prison my mail home might be interrupted and, anxious that my family should not be worried by lack of news, I arranged a cover-up. I wrote several cards, which I post-dated, and left them with a friend with instructions to post them at intervals while I was in prison. The plan miscarried. Somehow news reached home that I was in trouble. Fortunately, while we were denied parcels when in prison, we were allowed to receive and send out mail. I wrote explaining what had happened, trying of course to make light of it. I wrote rather confusedly for I was really quite distressed that my family had been informed, and possibly misinformed.

29.3.1943: Letter

In your latest letters you refer to my trouble. The letters lead me to believe that you know about my court-martial, presumably through the war office; but nothing further. I'd like to know the extent and source of your information. By the time you receive this letter, I will have finished my punishment.[1] I was sentenced to two months and one week imprisonment for trying to steal a small piece of cheese. As a result I've left the cheese factory as you probably already know. I had my court-martial in Danzig where for my defence I had a civilian lawyer. I then remained in Stalag HQ from the date of trial, Jan 19th, until I was sent to the special prison on March 4th. Should you receive 4 postcards post-dated to March 4th stating that I am still in Stalag HQ, these are only cards post-dated and posted by a friend of mine. I arranged that because I didn't consider it worth while mentioning a mere 2 months' sentence. As I say, I'll be out before you hear about it – so what's the use. If I couldn't endure 2 months' military punishment I would have been dead long ago. It's quite a pleasant change to have a date to

[1] The letter arrived 7 May and I was released 11 May.

which to look forward. Also very pleasant to leave XXB. In future address everything XXA. I'm allowed to write every third week – until May 11th, when I shall once again eat Red Cross, drink tea and smoke. Pleasant thoughts.

12.4.1943: Letter

There's really little to say. The most important point is that now, instead of counting the days in I'm counting the days yet to do. Four weeks today I'll be going out. By the time you receive this letter I'll once again be enjoying Red Cross parcels and a cigarette. Perhaps what I crave for most is a cup of tea. My private parcels are being held at Stalag XXA – there are already three American food parcels, three cigs and three book parcels waiting. It is really a novel experience to have a date of release, to know that on a certain day I'll be enjoying a change as great as passing from ordinary POW life to home life.[1] The people I'm sorry for are those who have two, three or four years, whose only hope is the end of the war. Fortunately we all believe that won't be long now. You can't imagine what ordinary POW life is like, much less how this life is. But be assured I'm in fine health although not so fat as usual and there's absolutely no need for anxious worry on your part. To me, it's just another experience fortunately limited, which I shall laugh at once I'm home.

These letters were written to provide reassurance. They naturally left a lot unsaid. It was indeed fortunate for me that my sentence was a relatively short one. The greatest hardship was perpetual hunger and the resulting weakness. Lack of food was compounded by a lack of cigarettes and tobacco. This did

---

[1] What an exaggeration that now seems to me.

not worry me so much, as I had never been a heavy smoker and had already given it up several times. But the greatest irritant, to me at least, was the impossibility of escape from the five others who were locked in with me. It was impossible to keep off the subject of food; there was always one of us spelling out his favourite menu. Moreover, one of the six was an argumentative Scot, from Glasgow. He was always contesting something or other, usually something of trivial importance. There were, for instance, fierce disagreements about the route of the No 11 London bus, a matter on which there was no method of proving one right and the other wrong. Many times I yearned for solitary confinement. The only relief from over-close confinement was when working outside the prison, although our weakness made this an additional ordeal. One did, however, see a few different faces. I remember the two Cypriots who told me about the beauty of their country.

I managed while in this prison to make a few notes on the envelope of a letter I had received from the Red Cross. What I wrote for my own eyes gives a more realistic portrayal than did my letters home of the time I spent in Graudenz prison.

18.4.1943: Diary

Today we are moving our quarters ... the change is for the worse. Our new cells are smaller, the beds three high and of iron and only a small window high up in the wall ... The last few days have taught me what weakness really is. My legs – oh, how they ached and protested against the weight of my body. The backs of my legs ached. It wasn't sheer exhaustion – it was something worse. I could just keep going but there was no hope of any relief. It was agony to shovel sand. I am feeling a wee bit stronger now. I haven't worked for three days on account of this move. On top of weakness I had stomach trouble. The five extra potatoes we received must have been in some manner unhealthy and also the soups. We

46

had what seemed like sea water one day. Over half the company suffered, some severely. Quite a number suffer from this weakness also. Easter brought some relief.

20.4.1943: Diary

I had a lovely surprise this morning. I had had four days inside. Marching to work I was delighted with the fresh greenness everywhere. I noticed sycamore trees in bud and even cherry blossom – the grass seemed incredibly green and looking down on the bushes bordering the river was a patchwork of light and darker greens. It was dazzling and the air was quite heavy with sap and perfume. Not such a pleasant sight were the hundreds of swastikas hanging from nearby windows. It was a rude gaudy shock as we were marched out of the prison gates this morning. However, we weren't sorry it was Hitler's birthday as we only worked three hours, starting late, finishing early and coming back to the prison at midday for dinner.

29.4.1943: Diary

I'm very impatient. I leave this detested prison a week on Monday and it cannot come quick enough. This is almost the worst period, comparable with the first fortnight – counting, counting each day. Everything else takes a back place, and even if I do manage to forget for a few minutes someone else enviously reminds me 'Well, it's not long now, Keith.'

Easter week-end was quiet enough but I'm afraid 95% of the workers wanted to get out after the first day. My four days were not so monotonous because I had a couple of books – *Wuthering Heights* and *Jane Eyre*. We were very fortunate with the *unteroffiziere* [NCO] on duty. The two who delight in ferreting out trouble were absent

47

(instead we have them all this week). It was very much more pleasant not to be on the alert all day, but to be able to lie peacefully on the bed...

Today I attended a burial parade. One of the lads died suddenly the day before yesterday – weak heart was certified. Under nourishment is nearer the mark. It was a simple affair – 14 men and our English captain to read the service. No German padre, no firing salute.

Well, back my thoughts wander to a week on Monday. How delicious certain foods taste in my imagination. Perhaps what I would like best is rice pudding ... thick and creamy. Another thing I want to realise quickly – to drink a tin of Nestle's milk. Enough, I'm only torturing myself. Just 14 days now. And then...

My final letter from Graudenz prison was written in a dream. I had received a letter saying that my father, sister and the children hoped to spend Easter on a farm near Welshpool (my great-grandparents came from Newtown).

4.5.1943: Letter

My thoughts were with you at Easter. Poignant memories of peaceful days on Welsh farms sharpened my imagination. As I woke on Good Friday morning before reveille, while everywhere was quiet, I heard a cock crow, very faintly in the distance, and instead of my cell, with bolted door and barred window, I could see a small farmhouse bedroom, softly white and oh, so clean like a scrubbed table, and the small deep-set window under the eaves, through which the sun slants. The fresh fragrance of an English spring morn permeated my cell. I could imagine opening the door and seeing the jug of hot water standing outside; and stepping downstairs into the clean fresh kitchen where bacon and eggs and lovely white farm bread and butter and, of course, the hot-cross buns awaited my appetite... I realise now where some of my happiest days were spent... I shall re-tour Wales. I become daily more attached to the countryside. I leave this prison in a week's time and after making up for lost time in eating and reading... I shall endeavour to have another spell on the farms this summer. After that may the war be over...

I also made some notes on my release from prison. One of my friends, Leslie Eyre, had arrived to start a sentence of three months, and he was able to pass on some news.

9.5.1943: Diary

Today [May 9th] has been even worse than yesterday. Although I couldn't concentrate to read yesterday, I did get the chance to chin-wag with Eyre. His interesting news of the latest court martial sentences took my mind off thoughts of the morrow and departure from this confinement and starvation. Surprising was Wilkinson's 5 years and Lester's 9 months and Forde's 2 months. Eyre also brought me the reassuring news that my fur-lined jack-boots had not been stolen. Ashton had them locked up and had now despatched them to Thorn to await my arrival there... Today has had little distractions in it. It has been one long patient wait. I woke at 5 o'clock, two hours before reveille. I tried reading, to no avail. I was up at 6:30 a.m. I was packed ready at 7:30. At 8:30 I moved over to 'E' Company into a large room with four Belgians as company. After battling gamely for nearly an hour to hold a conversation in school-boy French, of which all that was interesting was the news (official of course) that Africa was clear of German troops, I turned to amusing myself but only succeeded in walking the room and gazing out of the window. In the afternoon, I made vain efforts to be allowed to smoke (today being Sunday, a smoking day) and to attend the first church service given to the English here. A padre had come from Thorn.[1] I couldn't sleep. Dinner and tea made milestones, but hardly noticeable. I improved about 4 o'clock, passing over an hour learning by heart four poems I had copied out one time – Browning's *Home Thoughts from Abroad*, Addison's *Ode to Solitude* – a very different kind of solitude to mine – Shakespeare's '*Blow, Blow, Thou Winter Wind*', and Hardy's *Leisure* – but leisure capable of being employed. Later I played 'Battleships' with one of the Belgians (he won) proving once more how invaluable pencils are. Now I'm in bed at 8:30 p.m. and I'm not the slightest bit tired and despairing of sleep...

11.5.43: Diary

I'm in heaven. I'm sitting in the sun, reading an interesting book. Simple, but I'm ever so content. Perhaps it's the book, A G Street's *The Gentleman of the Party*, with its stories of the simple pleasures of farm life that made me suddenly realise what enjoyment, what naive pleasure I'm experiencing this moment. Contentment. I don't think it matters where one is, so long as there's contentment. How can anyone do better?

How I've enjoyed the past 24 hours. I left the prison at 10:05 am yesterday... As I ducked through the small door in the prison gates I looked up at the white concrete portal. There the black German eagle hovered over me and darkened my sense of release.

My immediate destination was the English working *kommando* in the town [Graudenz]... I was very disappointed – almost piqued – with my reception... I didn't expect to be petted but I did expect to be shown in and acknowledged. Like entering a hotel and finding no reception clerk or porter. When I did find the Sergeant-

---

[1] This may have been David Wild. He mentions visiting the prison.

Major I received a nod of the head, a cup of weak warm tea and two biscuits. I found consolation in the previous day's German newspaper, for I read of 'withdrawals from Bizerta and Tunis'. My heart warmed reading that; how long have we waited for it. How I longed to be with the boys.

Fortunately I had a voice and two legs, so I found myself a bed and the cook house. Two helpings of spuds and barley gravy went down well. Later on, when the S.M. gave me some Red Cross, I couldn't resist putting a bar of chocolate and a bowl of porridge in the same place. It was good food wasted, for I brought it all up half an hour later. I asked too much of my stomach.

Wandering round, enjoying my comparative liberty, I met Murtagh, one of my company whom I hadn't seen for 3 years. We had quite a pleasant chat exchanging news of other Cheshires we had met since our capture.

The evening was very enjoyable, I got chatting to the producer of a play coming off on Saturday, Sir John Irvine's *Antony and Anna*. I invited myself to the rehearsal. It's just my type of play – satirical humour... Later on, the band was in full swing – how music starved I am...

I was up with the light... 4.30 am, an hour before reveille. A cup of strong hot tea – oh! how grand it tasted, and by 5.30 am, in the fresh cool air, I was strolling round the football pitch. The best time of the day without a doubt, made especially enjoyable for me by an unavoid-able comparison with 24 hours previous. Freedom to stroll about in the open air. Freedom of the day, from a time table, to eat if I wished, to sleep or to read, to do this and not feel guilty of the wrong-doing – freedom from the jingle of keys and slamming of iron doors.

[Next day] How miserable life has become – all because the stomach rules. Fickle despot it is. Yesterday it again refused what I considered a moderate meal – fried meat roll, spuds and sauerkraut... As if that's not enough, I've tooth ache... Thank God I go to Thorn tomorrow morning.

51

4

Fort 13: A Different World

I travelled to Thorn on the 5 o'clock morning train, together with an English padre who had been visiting the *Kommando* at Graudenz. Having heard that Stalag XXA was well organised, I was curious about my return to Fort 13: what awaited me there, and the changes since 1940. I was, however, quite unprepared for what I discovered. It was a different world from all that I had known so far.

My first surprise was to find that the fort was apparently run, not by the Germans, but by our own officers and senior NCOs. We only saw the Germans at roll-call. In the following weeks, I was to discover that the fort, although still a transit camp for those on their way to or from some *Arbeitskommando*, had been made into a sort of cocoon or oasis by its more permanent residents.

Fort 13, in May 1943, was therefore a revelation. It was a place where I had time and opportunity to catch up with some of the things I had been missing, where the mind rather than the body was stretched, where one could seek out more congenial company and gain some privacy.

I lost no time in noting in my diary my change of fortune.

14.5.1943: Diary

Well, I'm in Thorn. My reception was very different from

that of the Graudenz Kommando ... It's too early for me to judge but the British seem to have complete control, a big contrast to Willenberg [Stalag XXB]. It certainly wasn't long before I was tucked up in bed on a water and milk diet. The doctor merely asked how long I'd been in prison and how much weight I'd lost. He was rather startled when I told him I'd lost 2 stone 5 lbs in 10 weeks.

Since the first weeks of June 1940, I've had exactly two days in a sick-bay. This, my second visit to Fort 13, is a repetition of the first only in the fact of immediate entry into the sick-bay. But then I was suffering from a fever, the result of a smallpox vaccination and a three day journey in a very overcrowded cattle truck. Since then I've had nearly 3 years' work and the clean cool sheets, the quiet sanctuary and unhurried comfort of a sick bay has attracted yet eluded me. I hadn't expected to be put in a sick-bay but that's the routine here with those from Graudenz now. But it was a rude shock to be ordered immediately to bed and refused any food ... I wanted to tour the fort, to see the changes since 1940, and above all to watch each face for there may be one or two I know ...

There are three Medical Orderlies in the room (10 patients) but they are unsympathetic. However, I've not had to suffer this starvation ... within a few hours of being forced to bed a man came in with an armful of parcels. He came a few minutes later with a second armful. It created quite an impression – 17 parcels, 3 of them food parcels from America. So under my pillow, out of sight, I have a box of soft sweet biscuits, a box of milk chocolates and I've just enjoyed an egg sandwich. There are over 1,300 fags for me and over a dozen books. Everything I need. Fortunately the orderlies have proved decent fellows and allowed me last night a plate of jelly and custard. If I prefer tea to milk I may. Needless to say I've tasted no water.

While in the sick-bay, my mind, no less than my body, craved for nourishment. Luckily, it was provided by Michael, a fellow patient who was suffering from a nervous breakdown. Although his account of life in the Fort proved to be exaggerated, I was regaled and beguiled by his conversation. It was, I recorded, 'the first intelligent conversation for months'.

22.5.1943: Diary

We discussed the British character, travel, books, life in the fort. Both of us very old and wise and most serious. But I did enjoy it. A man with a satirical pen has fine material in this fort. There is a social life as bad as any suburbia, with distinct grades of the social scale... One would think a POW camp the ideal material for communal living but the same trait that makes a man plant a privet hedge round his garden so that his neighbour cannot see his washing has here crystallised into a complex system of cliques and separate living quarters. There's the theatrical set, the boxing set, the musical set, the sporting set. And most incredible of all, all sorts of odd corners and bunkers, with which the fort abounds, have been converted into 'flats' ... these people ... are just as snobbish, just as hypocritical, just as jealous as any Mrs Boodlittle-Jones who has a West End address. From what Michael tells me if one set gets hold of a good book they keep it within their own circle. They'll ask you: 'Have you read so and so?' knowing full well they have the only copy... These flats are decorated most elaborately, and furnished with cushioned arm-chairs, table cloths etc., and they are more exclusive than any West End club... Most people are however 'frightfully bored' ...

I think this was more my companion, Michael, speaking than my observation. I had been less than ten days in the place, scarcely time enough to reach such conclusions. I painted a more favourable picture when I wrote home in mid-June. I was replying to a letter from my worried sister, who had just received news from me in Graudenz prison.

16.6.1943: Letter

I can't imagine what stories were rumoured about my case. POW camps are probably the worst breeding grounds for rumours. I understand it was Mrs Marshall who first brought you the news, having learnt from Harold, who in turn has heard it from goodness knows how many gossipers. As I said before it was actually so trivial that I didn't deem it worthy of mention. The transfer to this Stalag is full recompense. Here there's such a different atmosphere. It's a little bit of England. As contrasted to XXB the administration systems are greatly superior and the Germans don't interfere at all. The fort moat is now utilised as gardens and Middleton is the heathen god. He has hundreds of converts and his adherents are so fervent that they put in hours of work each evening, lettuce, onions, radishes, watercress, mustard seed (all English) is the economical result. Perhaps a materialistic religion but it adds essentially to the English atmosphere. The top of the fort is grassed over and on a hot sunny day resembles New Brighton; people basking in shorts, gramophones entertaining. Perhaps the deck chairs, paper bags and orange peel are absent, but all for the better. Played rugby for England here.

Nor did I find Fort 13 'society' so unapproachable as Michael had been suggesting. No doubt, many did find a Stalag HQ far too cliquish, especially those who were simply passing through on the way to and from an *Arbeitskommando*. As 'birds of passage', they missed what they had known on an *Arbeitskommando*, 'the sense of belonging ... overcome'.[1] For me, however, the company to be found in Fort 13 was much more

[1] Elvet Williams, *Arbeitskommando*, Gollancz, 1975, p. 141. W. R. Alderson found his Stalag to be 'one conglomeration of closely knit syndicates, which meant that one had to be in a hut a great length of time before being accepted as one of the boys'. *The Long Road Back*, Dorrance Publishing Co., 1994, p. 119.

congenial and I was soon able to report home that I had become part of an excellent quartet.

4.7.1943: Letter

... Thanks for all the sympathy. I've had a good rest.
I'm now on light work, still in Fort 13... I've found
new friends. I 'muck-in' with three others, two from
Brighton, the other from Jersey, a RAF chap. All good
companions, sharing my interests. We have some good
chats about school days... The Arts master of Rugby is
here, quite a good chap. I'm studying in earnest now –
an Oxford honours man is coaching me at German. I sat
the RSA-inter last month, and will sit the final next
month. I've written away about the CIS final, for in
winter I hope to have some spare time... I would have
done it before but I've never had less than 10 hours'
daily work and never the facilities. Of course, I may not
get the chance even now ... I've recovered all my
kit...

I had not anticipated such a long stay in Fort 13 – nine months.
I fully expected to be sent out on another *Arbeitskommando*, a
farm no doubt. It was, however, the British doctors who
decided whether or not I was fit and I had no objection to them
keeping me on the list of those deemed capable only of 'light
work'. It gave me time to discover new friends among the
'permanent residents': Denis Glover, a sergeant from the
Royal Sussex Regiment exercising his right not to work;
Alfred Honeycombe, an aircraftsman denied by German
policy any exit from the fort; and Len Harvey who, suffering
from an unending series of boils, required permanent medical
attention. My 'light work' took me outside the fort and
allowed me to engage in trade with the local population. I
bartered goods from our Red Cross parcels for items such as
fresh eggs or brandy. We were occasionally searched on
returning to the fort but it was only a disciplinary ritual.

56

Those searching us knew our art of concealment and we relied upon them carrying out their duties in a perfunctory fashion.

The longer I remained on 'light work', the more I was drawn into the life of the fort. I was included in the rugby team representing England in matches against the Scots and the Welsh. I helped in staging some entertainment. I set about studying for examinations. It seemed that the more active I thus became, the more I could count on postponing the day I would have to leave. It was becoming more and more obvious that I remained in Fort 13 not by chance but by the design of those who had the power to decide such matters, the officers and warrant officers who were effectively in charge. Some time later, I became aware of a hidden reason for my retention. An escape was being planned and my help was required.

The amenities of Fort 13 were, of course, no proof against 'Stalag blues', the ennui from which we all suffered. I allowed it to creep into my letters home all too often. I bemoaned the irregularity of incoming mail, forgetful of the earlier years when it was comparatively rare to receive a letter or a parcel. I voiced repeatedly my frustration and impatience, although I did certainly tone it down from what I wrote in my secret notes in August of that year:

Lazy wretch I am. No spirit, no initiative. It's a deadening existence. I realise that every day more and more, and my patience is short. It's time the war ended. Enough young life has been ended, and enough of my young years.

The danger is that of getting too comfortable. Better to be hungry and desperate. I'm tempted to join the bandits who live in the woods and annoy the Germans, picking off a policeman or a mayor here and there. Like Lawrence annoyed the Turks.

A few POWs did find that temptation irresistible. Among them was one of my Wallasey friends, Norman Cullity. That was not his only adventure. He was once on a working party which was put to work maintaining a stretch of railway line. This was being used to transport troops and war material. Three, one of them Cullity, refused to continue the work and were put before a firing squad. It was the ringleader who was targeted and he fell, badly wounded. The two others emerged unscathed but ended up in Graudenz prison.

2.9.1943: Letter

My mail has fallen off lately – only seven in August. Still I don't suppose there's much for others to say apart from Births, Marriages and Deaths... Already four years of war. But I mustn't bring reminiscences back – it makes me miserable. I must always think of the future but then that's so vague. So I live in the present, which is monotonous. Contrary to my expectations I shall not yet go on a working *Kommando* – still light work... I hope to send a photo with my next letter – England's rugger team. I enclose one here of a funeral I attended – of a chap who was with me last March–May (this is to say, Graudenz) – dysentery. I'm carrying the wreath – second row. In answer to Father's letter, we sleep inside the fort. Thirty to a room twice the size of the lounge, and skilfully decorated by ourselves; beds 3-high – clean and dry...

15.9.1943: Letter

... mail putrid: two this month so far. And how I miss it. Fortunately there's plenty of good news to compensate. It's a tonic but makes me so impatient. It's worse than stagnation, doing nothing to help. Repatriation has started, so I suppose Marshalls will be seeing Norman soon. Quite a few RAMC are going from here. Going home! It's such a realisation of everything, of all our hopes, dreams that have haunted us for over 3 years, that it's impossible to be excited. Just calmly unbelieving. I'll have to touch English soil before I realise it.[1] This week has been notable for the production of *Thark* – Ben Travers. Very well done and thoroughly enjoyable. There's a musical play in a fortnight's time – the leading lady has dropped out and they confronted me with the part. I've just been looking at the script. It's a bit weak and I don't like the idea. My German exam comes off next week-end – a 50–50 chance of a pass – inter-degree standard. I posted a photo of the English rugger side last week – it's separate. I hear Verity has died of wounds – a big loss to English cricket. I'll be 23 in a fortnight's time – pity I cannot be home for it. Remember I once thought I'd be home for my 21st. When the belated celebration does finally take place, all my guests will be married couples...

3.11.1943: Letter

Glad to hear of John's promotion.[2] Makes me feel rather out of it and realise how little I did... I'm learning shorthand now. Started Spanish but the teacher has returned home[3] – a sanitator. Am in a good variety show coming off this week-end. I'm composing a sketch etc. Also putting on a mock trial – my first personal management in a Stalag. I seem to fit into this place much better than the other [Stalag XXB]... Oh, how I ache for this war to end, so I can get back home. You get used to anything but a longing for home, and all that it means is ever present. The aggravating part is that we can do nothing to hurry on the end – just wait, wait, wait. Sorry

[1] There were rumours that long-term POWs might also be repatriated – never a very credible rumour.
[2] My brother, to captain.
[3] He was repatriated.

to be so weak, but although I'm really busy here, it's only a pretence. We sometimes laugh and forget.

17.11.1943: Letter

Nothing to acknowledge. Mail and parcels conspicuous by absence. Still they will turn up one day. We are now restricted to 30 lbs of kit, so until I send word, with exact requirements, don't send another clothing parcel. Please, however, continue to send fags. We had our first snow yesterday – a wet blizzard; and again today. The boots proving very useful, and quite a stir outside. How they marvel. Just been knocked out of the table-tennis tournament... We put on a show last week. I was composing a sketch; photographs were taken tonight but I had to play table-tennis and had a shorthand lesson, so had no time. I'm pretty busy here with one thing and another. Play quite a lot of contract [bridge] in the spare moments in between.

1.12.1943: Letter

Clothing parcel of 30 August received. Very many thanks; side-cap, shoes, gloves and underwear very useful. Also cap badge and brilliantine... I still don't know whether Norman has been repatriated or not... We are now allowed to send our camp money home – I may send some later. Can you send me *The Ship* recently published... The whole world now realises what war means. Cheerful, aren't I, but in this life everyone has spells of inertia and melancholy – the 'blues', which may last hours or days. I'm in one now, and shouldn't be writing a letter but the post goes tonight. Everyone else is talking of repatriation, but I have 'me doots' as the Scots say.

15.12.1943: Letter

Letters are rather rare these days... The *Mock Trial* I produced proved quite a success. I had only meant it for one night, because it was mainly impromptu in that no witness knew what questions may be asked and neither counsel knew the other counsel's case: they had knowledge of the plot and certain facts but the actual proceedings were impromptu. For the jury, I had persuaded Captain Cook, the dentist, and most of the sergeant-majors to join in; normally they would never have appeared on the stage, and they added to the farce. The first night was such a success that a repetition was requested. This was naturally more difficult to perform but went over all right. We're busy on the panto now, *Sinbad the Sailor*. The Christmas parcels have already arrived...

2.1.1944: Letter

Strange how I can look upon the beginning of another year almost with equanimity. At times, that is; often – very often, this life is as galling to me as ever. I've heard that one of the sanitators repatriated from here – I knew him – collapsed and died half-an-hour after the disembarkation... That's even more tragic than staying here. But I must tell you of Christmas ... good Christmas fare ... there was nothing lacking. Even the sauce for the pudding had that ingredient which makes all the difference[1] ... surprising how a little thing like a mince pie – actually I made 60 – gives cause for artistic pride but we have here so little outlet for individual creation – after all, building a German road or digging a hole is rather inadequate ... As in all previous Christmases, my thoughts

[1] It must have been brandy.

were with you, and the two RAF chaps who were moved to a RAF camp the week previous. I was very attached to them... My New Year wishes for health, happiness and peace, 1944. Year of Victory...

5

A Brief Escape

The new year did not bring peace but if offered me the next best thing – the chance of making a successful escape. This came my way when I was asked to help in the escape of two RAF personnel, using one of the escape routes reserved for those whose war-time skills gave them priority. I had heard vaguely of such escape routes, labelled enviously 'the armchair route'.[1] My role was to be that of escort. Lucky me! We were to be provided with false papers, civilian clothes, money, and on arrival in Danzig we would have some local help in boarding a Swedish ship. Once in Sweden nothing could stop us reaching home. Home at last! My spirits soared.

Unfortunately, it did not turn out as I had anticipated. I was told a little later that something had happened to the escape route, much reducing the chances of success. Consequently, the planned escape was cancelled, and I was no longer needed as an escort. However, if I wished to take my chances on my own, a getaway would be arranged as originally planned. This would probably get me to Danzig, and some local help might still be available there. Did I wish to make the attempt? It might have crossed my mind that during many months spent

---

[1] The volume of the *Official History of New Zealand in the Second World War* entitled *Prisoners of War* states that a British and a New Zealand officer made a successful escape from one of the forts of Stalag XXA on 9 October 1943.

close to Danzig in 1941, I had always discounted the chances of getting on board ship. Objectively my chances of success had probably not much improved, apart from having learnt to speak German fluently, but that was now irrelevant. It was a different moment and I was in a different mood. I was all keyed up to go and had no hesitation in saying so.

The preparations let me into some of Fort 13's secrets, although no further than was necessary. My photograph needed to be taken for the identity card. It was done very professionally within the fort. In due course I was given my *Ausweis* (identity card) with my false identity, but the means whereby it was produced, good enough to pass inspection, were not revealed to me. I was measured for my civilian clothes but had no idea how the material was obtained. I was given some money. I asked no questions; not even about how my escape was to remain undetected for 24 hours. I was to leave the fort one morning, in exactly the same way as on many a previous day – that is, with a working party detailed to do some work in the vicinity of the town, Thorn. My failure to return with the working party would not be discovered – or rather, would only be disclosed – at morning roll-call the following day. I have often wondered how it was done. My only personal contribution to the preparations was the making of a small plywood case with a false bottom, where I stored some chocolate. Not knowing the circumstances in which I might find myself, I thought it prudent to have something nourishing in reserve.

It was early February – still winter – when I walked out of the fort, full of hope and having said farewell to the few who were in the know. Some time before we were due to finish work, I slipped away to a pre-arranged hiding place, up in the rafters of a shed. The plan was to remain there most of the night, and then, before dawn, don the civilian clothes, walk to the railway station, purchase a ticket, and catch the early morning train to Danzig.

All went well. The station was crowded with passengers, and nobody took any notice of me. But when seated in the train, packed shoulder to shoulder, those on either side of me began to complain about my coat. It was of a fluffy material and some of the fluff was coming off on to their clothes. I made do with an apology and pretended to sleep.

In a few hours I arrived at Danzig. I had been given the name and address of a Pole to contact. He was not expecting me and was not at home when I knocked on his front door. It was still daylight and I was asked to come back in the evening, after dark. I filled in the time by going to the cinema. There I made the mistake of lighting up a cigarette. I was unaware that smoking in cinemas was forbidden. The usherette immediately appeared and ordered me to extinguish my cigarette. I was left wondering whether that was the end of the matter or whether, when the lights came on for the interval or at end of the film, something else awaited me. Fortunately not, and I was free to hurry away.

My meeting, later that evening, with my Polish contact confirmed what I had been given to expect: that I would have to rely upon my own devices rather than count on anything that could be arranged for me. I had the impression that my arrival was perhaps inopportune and that it was a time for lying low. As it was already late, the immediate problem was that of having somewhere to spend the night. It was decided to take me to somebody else's house, where I made my first acquaintance with a duvet. Blanket-less, sheet-less, pyjamas-less, I slept very well.

My chances of boarding a ship depended, in the first place, on gathering some information about the docks, how to gain access, and the location and movement of Swedish ships. I began to reconnoitre and, in the course of doing so, came across some British POWs at work. I had an idea. I could solve my problem of having somewhere to eat and sleep safely if one of the men on the working party wanted to spend the night outside. It was not unusual for POWs to climb out of camp, in order to enjoy a few hours of liberty, preferably in the company of a Polish girl. To change places with me for the night would no doubt be a welcome proposition. We could change clothes and identities, shortly before the end of the working day, and again in the morning.

65

This was soon arranged and so I found myself, quite unexpectedly, once again marching through the gates of a POW camp. Fortunately it was a large one, and there was very little risk of an unfamiliar face being detected. It was a most odd sensation to be on the run and yet to be standing on parade for roll-call and to be counted by an unsuspecting German guard. There were several British officers in charge. I reported to them, and I was entrusted with some information to take back home. It was the location of coastal batteries.

I might have given myself more of a chance of passing on that information had I been more circumspect. I had found an easy way of approaching the dockside where Swedish vessels were tied up, but it was not one I could use in reverse. I was taking my chance on a single throw. It might have been wiser to have given myself more time to weigh up alternative ways of getting on board, and of returning, perhaps in daylight when the dock would not have been so deserted. Against that had to be weighed the possibility of some mishap depriving me of even a single chance. I was learning how easily mishaps could occur. I had already nearly slipped up in the cinema by smoking. I had also experienced an awkward moment in a post office when sending a telegram to my contact. I had not been expecting the question, shot at me very quickly by the lady at the counter – *dringendes oder einfaches*? She wanted to know whether the telegram was to be sent at express or ordinary rate – fortunately a question which quite naturally might require a moment's reflection. I hesitated, unsure what was meant, then, recovering my wits, answered '*einfaches*' – ordinary rate. I concluded that, on balance, the sooner I attempted to get on board ship the better.

Access to the dockside was by dropping from a road bridge spanning the railway track used by the trains travelling to and from the quayside. It was relatively simple to drop on to one of the wagons. But once done there was no going back. Since it was a case of now or never, I had discarded the civilian clothes and destroyed my identity card, but kept the chocolate. I had chosen night-time rather than daytime, because I thought that would give me more cover. I made my way to the quayside

66

and from my hiding place I could see – and it was a wonderful sight – a Swedish boat, its dimly lit gangway inviting me on board. I could see no sign of a sentry, nor was anybody else in sight. Although it all looked a bit too quiet, almost unreal, it seemed that here was my chance, and I took it. But, as I moved out to cross the open ground which lay between me and the gangway, from somewhere there appeared an armed guard. There was no possibility of bluff – I was, after all, in uniform. I thought of attempting to overpower him and of pushing him into the dock, but then the hunt would be on for me and there was no escaping it.

The next day I was interrogated. It was my first experience of the more subtle forms of questioning. I was expecting the usual storm of verbal abuse, even physical assault. I was merely asked to explain how I had escaped, made my way to Danzig and entered the docks. My story, obviously invented, was not contested. I was taken in by the unexpected civility of the officer interrogating me and should have been more on my guard when, in the course of some further conversation, Coulthard's name was mentioned. It was assumed that I knew him and I did not deny it. He had been helping in my preparation for the RSA examination in German but he had also had a hand in my escape, by supplying the name and address of the Polish contact in Danzig. I should have realised that he was under suspicion. Shortly afterwards, he was moved from Fort 13 to elsewhere in Thorn.[1]

It was also the end of my stay in Fort 13. After a short spell of punishment for having attempted an escape, I was once again on my way to an *Arbeitskommando*.

---

[1] Tony Coulthard was a corporal in the Intelligence Corps. He had organised several escapes. He once reached the Swiss frontier and had actually passed through the German Border control but had turned back to assist his two companions, who were being questioned. He died in March 1945 while still a POW. (See p. 85)

6

Back to Work

To be back on an *Arbeitskommando* was bound to feel like exile. Fort 13 had been a haven, providing congenial company, interesting conversation, some leisure, opportunities to study, to read, to earn a place on stage or on the playing field – in short a civilised environment. Having spent nearly three years in various work camps and nine moths in Fort 13, I was in a position to compare the two worlds and I had no doubts about which I preferred. But I had no choice, only a memory, constantly recalled in my letters home.

19.3.1944: Letter

... I'm on a farm now but hope to return to Stalag HQ soon. I have had a pleasant nine months there (although we lost the two RAF chaps before Christmas)... The library made a very cosy retreat for our little family – a little privacy and space and quiet, otherwise impossible. We had just made an excellent sofa out of Red Cross cases and packing. And an oven to bake my pastry. However a welcome is always there for me if I do return. Comfort, intelligent conversation, friendship, study and sport have made these nine months the best of my stay here. My only regret was that Toss and Les weren't with me. The result of my RSA German final is not yet through... If I get back to Stalag I'll start on the final CIS.

I did not last very long on this first *Arbeitskommando*. It was not a large camp, about 20 men, including several NCOs who had volunteered to work like the rest on the surrounding farms. All had been there for several years and had become part of the local community, the war more or less forgotten. There was only one guard, Everybody, so it seemed, had taken full advantage of the opportunity, when out working and free from observation, of establishing a cosy relationship with some of the women. I must have been seen as a meddlesome intruder, for I certainly did not share their apparent devotion to work or their uncritical acceptance of living quarters which were far too cramped. In speaking out, I upset the guard, my employer on the farm and my fellow POWs. I felt out of place, and saw no hope of finding there a kindred spirit, so I was not sorry when I was told to pack my kit. My departure was a blessing all round.

I was taken back to Fort 13 but unfortunately not for long. I was soon sent off to another working party. My diary comments on the change.

29.4.1944: Diary

I must compare this *kommando* with Ribenz, where I spent four weeks in March. That was my first *kommando* in this Stalag [XXA]. It came abruptly after nearly a year of Fort 13 life. The contrast was too great, the pull of the Fort's amenities and my friends there too strong. I could only see the disadvantages of the place. I suppose I'd made up my mind to be dissatisfied with the place. I did a lot of 'shit-stirring'. One sergeant packed his kit and went where he belongs.[1] The billet was far too small –

---

[1] That is, with the others who had exercised their right not to work.

also the windows. It wasn't the billet, however, which was extended – the commando was reduced by 3 men, and I was one of them. I still have the guard's threat of '*Straf-kompanie*' [punishment-block] ringing in my ears – for he was convinced I was lazy – but he must have wondered a little as I strode – almost ran – through the fort gates without deigning to look back at him trailing behind.

My diary continued:

I had an excellent Easter week-end in the fort – a show, a booze, a game of rugger. My spirits were high as I arranged for a job in Stalag gardens, and as I got into bed that afternoon I was visualising a peaceful summer of little work and much sunbathing amid the intellectual company of books and my friends. But a guard came and brought me here, to Grossschönbruck. Something had gone wrong and it was another farewell. On the train here I accepted temporary defeat and decided to make the best of it. I stepped through the billet door with a less dissatisfied, less prejudiced spirit than when I arrived at Ribenz. When I saw three rooms, and in my room only three other men and a fair amount of bed space, I was even less discontented, and in the morning, after a tour of several of the farms – it is single farms here – I resigned myself to making this my home for a while and to be a fairly well-behaved POW.

In fact, apart from a short midsummer break spent in Fort 13, Grossschönbruck was to be my 'home' for the rest of 1944 and into the new year. There I was once more caught in the daily deadening routine of an *Arbeitskommando*. There were a few minor compensations, some of which I mention in my letters home. But there was no disguising the tedium of this final year. The landings of the Allies in France were a tonic, as was news from the Eastern front. But strangely, the prospect of being home by Christmas did not so much ease the tedium as aggravate it. We had long learned patience and now we were becoming impatient.

5.6.1944: Letter

My news will go in two lines, so you can judge that fundamentally and particularly, it is just the same. Farming, and finding the one day of rest very precious...

I picked up *Tom Brown's Schooldays* last night. I've just finished it. It made much more of an appeal to me than I thought it would and rather thanked the cloudy sky. The weather is so changeable – mostly rain, sometimes cold. But last week-end, which was Whit, it was a heat-wave. I went swimming. Glorious. Our camp is almost surrounded by lilac trees – it makes me think of lilacs at home. The cherry blossom is finished long ago; even the apple blossom is falling. When I see cherry blossom I think of the Moselle Valley where I spent March '40. That was lovely country, so different from northern France. The spring was so glorious after that terrible winter...

In late July, I was briefly back in Fort 13. I have neither record nor recollection of why I was recalled: it was no doubt to sit my examination in Advanced German. On my return to Grossschönbruck I found myself no longer working on one of the farms but in the local dairy. As I wrote home, there were distinct advantages.

1.8.1944: Letter

I'm back on commando. I didn't return to my old farm but I'm in the dairy. It's a big improvement. I know how much work I have to do: it's hard while it lasts; then I've a couple of hours of quiet in which to read. The food is excellent, everything's in season at the moment, vegetable and fruit which we need most. I make the cheese – nothing like Cheshire. It means working Sunday mornings, but it's worth it. Much better than farming. Reading an excellent book, *Oliver Wiswell* by Kenneth Roberts of *Northwest Passage* fame. I was hoping to take part in the sports at Stalag next Sunday – 100, 200, 500, 1000, 4000 metres, putting the shot, long jump, high jump, discus and tug of war. Today I've been swimming – water lovely and warm, and then a sleep in the sun. The one advantage over Stalag.

Just two of us worked in the dairy. The day began with the arrival of the milk from the surrounding farms, in large churns on horse-drawn carts. There was a machine to separate the cream but all the rest was done by hand, even the making of the butter. The cheese was made in a long open vat. I had to warm the milk to the required temperature, add the rennet and then, when the milk had curdled, carve it like a cake, whisk and sieve it. The cheeses, wrapped in muslin, were left to drain and the afternoon was spent, more leisurely, periodically turning them over and cleaning up, ready for the next day. It was a daily routine into which I became settled for the rest of the year, waiting like the rest of the world for the end of the war.

1.10.1944: Letter

... My birthday past. I had a nice cake made. Winter time comes in tonight... Red Cross parcels are now one a fortnight but I get very good rations at the dairy so that's no worry. Cigarette parcels are non-existent, but they will come through some time... I'm just carrying on, work, a little reading, and sleep. I'm thankful for books. Reading some Aldous Huxley at the moment. Hope there's a speed up now that we've reached Switzerland... Waiting, like all the rest of the world.

6.10.1944: Diary

An uneventful three months. No newly developed thoughts, opinions. There's been no time, no peace. Work, a little reading, bed. What have I read? Another version of *Heloise and Abelard* by George Moore, *On the Margin* by Aldous Huxley, a 1943 American 3rd rate novel *Paper Houses* by William Plomer, *Brazilian Adventure* by Peter Fleming, *Human Psychology*, *Oliver Wiswell* by Kenneth Roberts. Not much for nearly 3 months.

No time, no peace. I was thinking not of the distant war but of the bedlam which awaited me each day on return from work – endless talk in loud voices on matters of no interest to me, and from which there was no escape. The next day was, however, a Sunday. Everybody went out so I had the room to myself and let my mind wander.

7.10.1944: Letter

I dedicate this letter to Nancy and Bee,[1] for it was you who taught me my enjoyment this afternoon. When you read it, I hope you won't think it a waste of a letter. I have the camp to myself, itself an enjoyment all too rare. So I've squatted down on the rug in front of the fire, and toasted myself a couple of crumpets and made a pot of tea. And I've 'wasted' the whole afternoon, just gazing into the fire. But how calmly content. It's getting dark but I won't draw the curtains, switching on the light would reveal the harsh reality. And here I've sat, done nothing, thought nothing, till really I must get something done. I've even let the fire go out, or very nearly. You know these afternoons, don't you? But the harsh reality: the fire is a stove. There are no curtains for me to leave undrawn,

---

[1] My sister and an aunt.

no brilliant electric light, only a carbide lamp which doesn't burn properly. The crumpets were sardines on toast but well buttered and peppered. But I've rested my mind even if I've scorched my shins – bad for me but didn't we scorch them at home? A fire is a wonderful comforter, especially in the autumn in the dark; the flickering coals and shadows dope the mind, hypnotise us into a peaceful, restful blank. Until we realise the fire is out and we've lots of things to be done. Once more, rush, worry, rush. Thank you, Nancy and Bee for a lovely afternoon.

22.10.1944: Letter

... We had a visit from the IRC [International Red Cross] the other day, who told us no more clothing parcels were being sent... Sorry I wasn't on the repat. ships, but you should have seen Miles by now, who went with that batch, and had some first-hand news of me. Life on the dairy continues as usual. The limitation of parcels to one a fortnight has no effect on me except the tea is not so plentiful. I get very good rations – all fresh food. Out here is certainly healthier for me than Stalag; but I miss my friends, the leisure and Stalag amenities. Like you we merely wonder 'how long' now that we can see the possibility of a finish. But don't be too confident. I know time slips by so swiftly; when we stop to realise exactly how long has been consumed in pleasure-less war we are horrified; but it could still last many months. The fag parcels are coming through once again. I got 3 this week.

For the next three months – the final three months in Grossschönbruck, as uneventful as the previous three – correspondence home focused on the Germans, retreating out of France and out of Russia. We were often out of step with those at home, because of the time lag in our correspondence – several months between writing and receiving a reply. The news of Allied advances, which had elated my family, had, by the time I received the letters, been superseded by more sobering news. I kept a more even keel, having learnt not to hope too wildly. As the war dragged on, my thoughts turned to preparation for Christmas – surely the last. I would have liked to have spent it with my friends in Fort 13.

5.11.1944: Letter

A batch of letters arrived yesterday. One from Nancy, Sept 7th, which showed me how the victories of France and Eastern Europe tricked you into the most optimistic optimism. We felt much the same here but then – well, I've learnt not to be too optimistic about anything; and we always hear the other side.

...July's clothing parcel for which I thank you gratefully. The white shirt is lovely: such a change to khaki. There's a lot of change to Royal Sovereign and Venus pencils; and in Utility Gilette blades. That's the rub of a total war: it affects the little comforts...

I have moved into the top room (there are 3) of this house, where we are only 6 and very much quieter. I've procured a single wire bed, and a feather pillow so I can lie in comfort and read in peace now. Incidentally, *War and Peace* has just arrived. Should you be able to get *This Above All* by Eric Knight you might like it, Nancy. But it may be banned, the language is coarse and the criticism of many things English strong...

19.11.1944: Letter

Mail slack but a parcel... Letters are arriving quicker now: sometimes within 3 weeks of posting. Our thoughts are on Christmas and the preparations thereto... It is most unfortunate I shall not be with my Stalag friends this year ... [they] ... helped last Christmas to be the most successful in this life... Stalag is not such a pleasure home at the moment. A parcel a fortnight makes the menu meagre, and the new camp, barracks, are in a very exposed spot to the wind. We have already had snow ... and I'm wearing the boots already. Here I have plenty to eat and a warm billet for we forage in the nearby woods for fuel. But spiritually I'll be poorer for I haven't a close friend here. It is a great pity Toss and I were separated. We spent the difficult days together – the test of friendship. I can count on six life-long friends...

3.12.1944: Letter

Nancy's of 23/10 received. So sorry you were so optimistic, for the disappointment will have been all the greater. It was heart-breaking to read your letters, so confident that I had my kit packed, that the war was really over. We also had great hopes and after each disappointment we hope anew, but always a patient hope. So I continue working in the dairy and write you the fortnightly letter. We are busy preparing for Christmas but it will be difficult this year as there is no Red Cross, unless supplies come in quickly. And very little to smoke. Myself I shall have an excellent dinner and I've held fags back from when I received a rush of parcels but I'm thinking of the 'family' in Stalag... I'm in good health and have put on 13 lbs since July – I'm now 12 and a half stone...

1.1.1945: Letter

As we saw the New Year in one thought was uppermost in all our minds – and probably yours also. Is this the last year? A year is the limit of thought of the future. The past year seemed to have passed quickly, there are so few outstanding events to mark the time. It's difficult to realise the actual span between '39 and '45. I've had no word from you for over a month now. Everything is held up, including Red Cross. Christmas was a little unreal to me this year, for in the dairy I had to work every day, until about 1 or 2 o'clock. I should love a lie-in some morning. Reading is still my only recreation. I could perhaps have done a little ice-skating but I felt more like lying in bed. Everything is covered in white. It's a steady 10–15 degrees C below now-a-days. That's not cold unless there's a wind. Against that there's no protection but, of course, I'm indoors ... Our home-made pies were a success judged by the speed with which they disappeared. The Christmas pudding unfortunately we couldn't make because we had no suet.

7

Taking Stock and a Change of Mind

That was the last letter my family received. One, written a fortnight later, went astray. This was just as well, for it would have certainly surprised and puzzled them. It announced, but scarcely explained, a radical change in my post-war plans. For this reason, I had copied it into my diary.

15.1.1945: Diary

I'm now finally convinced that I want to use my life in contemplation. Had I returned from France, become an officer, I may have been set for an active life in business or trade, for then I would have been accustomed to command and organise and would enjoy the not-to-be-neglected advantages of officer status which opens many a door in this class world. So I'm already handicapped in the economic race. But more important, the preference is a long last belief in my wish and capability for contemplation. I hope to have a period at 'varsity, in perhaps philosophy and modern history. I realise of course I need money for this, so I intend, as a first and essential step, to write a book (which is already planned). Pecuniary reward is a poor reason for writing but I have also the essential reason that I have something to write. Success or failure ... it must be tried... It is at last something I want and that promises success.

It would have been more informative had I added, to the negative reasons for discounting my chances in the business world, some more positive explanation for wanting to study philosophy and for being drawn to a life of contemplation. But the reasons, which had been occupying my mind for several months, were not easily condensed into a short letter.

A change in my plans for the future came about when, looking back on four years of captivity, I evaluated them afresh. Hitherto, in my letters home and in my diary, I had portrayed them as wasted years. I had been plagued by the thought that for me, but not for others, life was standing still, that I was missing out on the opportunities offered by life, even in wartime, for self-advancement, professionally and socially. I was assuming that I would be returning to work for ICI and that I would complete the Chartered Institute of Secretaries examinations. From that point of view, four years as a POW did seem a complete waste. While it was perhaps useful to have acquired a knowledge of German, I placed no value whatsoever on having learnt how to use a shovel, a pickaxe, a hoe or even on knowing how to make cheese or milk a cow. I had no use for the 'skills' of a manual labourer.

This was, of course, a blinkered point of view. Life was not standing still and I was not merely marking time. I had recognised this in a letter written seven months earlier while farming at Grossschönbruck.

21.5.1944: Letter

...I've finished one life, am having a visit to hell where I'm learning and experiencing a lot that's good and, if I'm not careful, also a lot that's harmful, and afterwards I'll start a new life. Family ties, or shall I say loves, will be the only connection. Love, hate, sufferance, impatience, occasional enjoyment, very occasional excitement, comradeship and solitude, all have a part in me here. Details are best left. I believe your present life is much the same. My hands are still farming, setting potatoes just recently. I suppose my mind is scarred like they are; but both are probably more useful; but both need recreation...

This letter not only left out details; it also skated over the deeper waters of self-knowledge. What in my letter I called a scarring of the mind was in fact a loss of self-esteem. I was feeling irretrievably debased by what I had experienced. I had written in my diary, a few days earlier:

14.5.1944: Diary

I can realise now the value of self-honour. But I have only realised it at the loss of some of my own self-honour. Like appreciating home when I'd left it. I wonder if the pure realise how envied they are. How I envy my former self, for with each day that I live I am guilty of some petty meanness or impure thought. No swing of the pendulum in the opposite direction can compensate. What is it, the soul or the conscience?

The explanation for wanting to study philosophy and live a life of contemplation lay in that question. What within me had prompted this *cri de coeur*? I wanted to know. I recognised the commands of conscience, but on what grounds? Was it because I had been brought up in a certain way? Was it intuitive? Was I right in my judgement of what was right and what was wrong? Having abandoned any belief in Christian doctrine, I could not settle for any Christian answer – but an answer had to be found.

It was perhaps not entirely fortuitous that I had come to ask such questions at that particular moment. Four years had gone by in unaccustomed situations and unfamiliar company. I had been forced to come to terms – and in some matters had refused to do so – with aspects of life which I found revolting, degrading, dispiriting. Four years as a POW had made me more aware of, but also uncertain about, my inner self. Although no end was yet in sight – the landings in Normandy had not yet taken place – it was time to take stock. The potato field was as good a place as any for resolving my queries and composing my vision of the future. The intellectual and emotional void of near-slavery invited not only fantasies of tea and crumpets in front of an autumn fire; it also opened the door to self-examination. The mind, disengaged from hands setting the potatoes, was free to roam. It swept aside any lingering concern I might have had for lost opportunities in the business world and became focused on the much more important question, how was I to judge the moral deterioration which had undoubtedly occurred within me during the past four years?

The short spell back in Fort 13 in midsummer was providential. It gave me access to a library where I might find some guidance compatible with my own line of thinking and to companions with whom I could discuss such matters. One of them, Len Harvey, was especially helpful. His scepticism was a perfect foil for the formulation of my own convictions. I noted in my diary two of the books which struck a chord.

26.6.1944: Diary

I've just read Stephen Foot's *Life Began Yesterday* – his experience and praise of the Oxford Group. I wish to have a 'quiet time' and note my opinions. It's the Christian religion with a new appeal to suit the hard-headed sceptical 20th-century citizen. Eternal life in heaven has been the reward to a Christian, unknown, unknowable. Hell-fire has been the penalty to a heretic, likewise unknown, unknowable. The true Christian had to face ridicule, perhaps poverty, discomfort to win eternal life. How many have chosen the easier life on just as good a gamble that there's no eternal life. The Oxford group promises a reward in this life; the loss of fear, a purpose to live, a new hope, a new confidence, happiness. The instinct to worship demands a religion; here's a good one, a good investment. There's some return in this life and should there be a next life, well, that's even better.

The basic tests of absolute honesty, absolute purity, absolute unselfishness, absolute love are ideal moral standards. But why bring in the Christian God? The *Quiet Time* when guidance is needed is not communion with God but with our own conscience.

Len had given me one of his poems to read which expressed his nihilism. I was trying to write a poem of my own which answered his but was having difficulty in selecting and writing my thoughts. Tolstoy came to my rescue.

7.7.1944: Diary

... Late in the evening I picked up Tolstoy's essay *What is Art?* and started to read it. It is very rare that I pick up a book which fits exactly to my mood. I knew immediately this is the most perfect case of harmony I've so far experienced. His discussion of subject matter and form had the effect of filling up the jig-saw fragment I had juggled with all day. I can hardly find disagreement on any one point – merely that he seems too much a Christian (in his own sense)...

... the greatest tragedy in life is when a man kills his soul before he starts to think on life. In such a case he has no soul to guide his doubts. He can only reason to accept the world and consider himself and all his generation quite justified in practising what I would call an unjust life, a life of sensation based on an evil nature oblivious to noble action or emotion...

I was nearer to Christian doctrine of the Fall than I realised –

but still lacking the essential revelation of redemption. I did not call my faults 'sins' but in envying purity I was in effect recognising them as such. When I drew up a balance sheet at the end of the year, noting that whereas knowledge and experience had benefited, my moral assets had continued to depreciate. I was still using my secular terminology but it was a form of confession.

Inevitably, I also reviewed my attitude to war, and concluded that 'patriotism is an evil passion'. I recognised the right of self-defence against 'undeserved aggression' but, I argued to myself, 'modern war does not mean this'. It was mutual slaughter. I recalled how, at the annual Cenotaph service which I attended with my father, 'the carved names appeared to be not heroes but unfortunates'. Recalling the exchange of pupils between my school, Wallasey Grammar School, and the Oberrealschule of Zehlendorf, Berlin, I wondered 'what could not be done by the youths of nations meeting'. I asked myself whether it might not be better to be a conscientious objector. I was torn by doubt rather than by conviction. Three months later when I next wrote in my diary I had still not resolved the question.

6.10.1944: Diary

I have been gazing wistfully at the family photo sent out to me. I can always spend a minute or two studying it, often longer, for my mind goes back. I like looking at Father. He's a grand old man but then the thought occurs. Suppose he had to suffer a German invasion like the Poles suffered. I thought of one particular youth here who lost his father murdered. He is one of thousands. The full tragedy of such a horrible loss to this youth has only just occurred to me, for until now I have thought of the thousands, not of them as individuals. The mind cannot grasp the true meaning of large numbers. A thousand gives a faint impression but one old man, how vividly can I imagine the horror of it all. It makes me dread the thought of my Father having to suffer what many other fathers suffered.

By January 1945, it had become obvious that I could not unaided find the answers to all that was puzzling me. As the war was clearly coming to an end, it was time to make up my mind. The result was my letter of 15 January – to give up the career I had started with ICI prior to the war, to study philosophy at a university, and to finance myself by writing.

8

The Winter March Homewards

The final ten weeks of captivity were almost the worst, matching in physical and mental exhaustion my ten weeks in Graudenz prison. It had never occurred to me that we would be forced, at the very end of the war, to march out of Poland and across northern Germany, in temperatures well below zero, never knowing where we would spend the night, in the snow or in a barn, nor whether we would be given anything to eat, nor what might be our ultimate destination. It was most providential that I had spent the last five months of 1944 working in a dairy indoors. The good food and the warmth helped me to survive this final test.

We were forced to march deep into Germany because the Russians had broken through the German defences. The direction, and still more the speed of the ensuing breakout, had taken everyone by surprise. The German Army had been defending, at the end of 1944, a line which ran, in the north, close to the eastern frontier of East Prussia; in the centre, through the middle of Poland; and, in the south, through Hungary and Yugoslavia. The Russians were still not on German soil.

Hitler gave priority to the defence of Hungary, where Budapest was under siege. Hungary was the one remaining source of oil and an important supplier of grain. But he left the line all the way from East Prussia to the Carpathian mountains dangerously overstretched. General Guerdian's request, that it

85

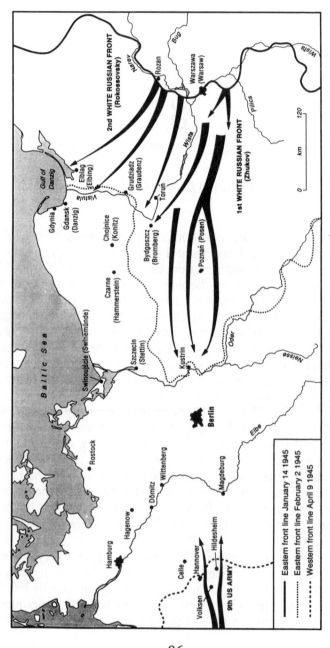

The Russian Advance, January 1945, and the American 9th Army Advance, April 1945

Legend:
— Eastern front line January 14 1945
····· Eastern front line February 2 1945
---- Western front line April 9 1945

be reinforced by transferring the 26 divisions serving relatively little purpose in Estonia and Latvia, had been rejected. Moreover, the 6th Panzer Army, transferred from the Western front after the Battle of the Bulge, was sent not to reinforce Army Group Centre but to Hungary.

When the Russians launched their attack on 12 January 1945, it was Army Group Centre which bore the brunt of it. Forbidden to withdraw and lacking adequate reserves, it could not stem the Russian advance. While General Koniev headed for the industrial area of Upper Silesia, Generals Zhukov and Rokossovsky made for Berlin and the Baltic. Stalags XXA and XXB lay in the path of Zhukov's right flank advancing on Torun and Bydgoszcz and Rokossovsky's left flank pushing towards Marienburg, Elbing and Danzig. The breadth, depth and speed of their advance – Zhukov had reached Bydgoszcz on the 23rd, an advance of over 160 kilometres in one week – not only threw the Germans into near total disarray: it also confronted us POWs with a dilemma. It provided, perhaps, the opportunity to escape and await liberation by the Russians – freedom at last. On the other hand, our evacuation which the Germans had ordered would take us towards the British and American armies advancing from the West. Our liberation would be postponed but it would take place much nearer home.

It was not so much a choice as a gamble. We had no reliable means of knowing how close the Russians were, nor whether the Germans would be making a stand on the lower Vistula, a natural barrier linking Torun, Graudenz, Marienburg and Danzig. When, on January 20th we were ordered to pack up and move out, I was undecided. But I calculated that, if I were to gamble on liberation by the Russians, I would need to make my escape while still east of the river. Once across the bridge at Graudenz, it would probably be too late. Our camp being only 33 kilometres from Graudenz, a decision had to be taken more or less immediately.

Had I known what the evacuation was to entail, I would not have started on the march westward. Escape would not have been too difficult in the circumstances and the local Poles

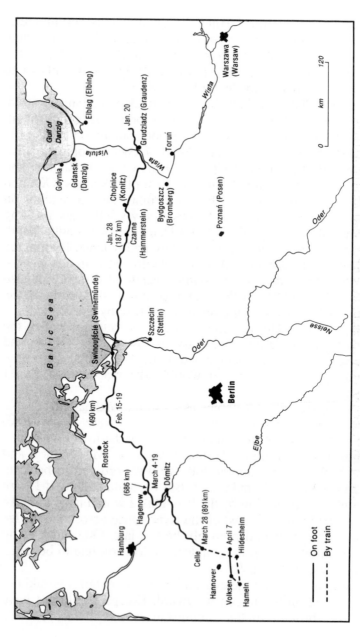

The Winter March out of Poland, 20 January to 7 April 1945

would have provided a hiding place. But the thought that I might well find myself trapped between opposing armies was the decisive factor.[1] At the end of the following day, after a 26-kilometre march, I was crossing the bridge. Its length – it must have been several hundred metres – gave me ample time to wonder whether I was really making the right decision, but by then the die had been cast.

Once across the river, there seemed no alternative but to keep going. We were expecting to be crammed into cattle trucks, as in 1940, but we were part of a general exodus, outnumbered by the German civilian population streaming out of East Prussia and the Polish corridor into Pomerania and Mecklenburg, their ultimate destination perhaps no more certain than ours seemed to be. They likewise were being obliged to travel on foot – there was no other way. What they feared was our hope: to be overtaken by the Russians. Rumours abounded as usual; it was believed that some columns of POWs had been liberated by Russian troops only to be recaptured in a German counter-attack! In fact, some of the POWs evacuated from Torun, and marching towards Bydgoszcz, were liberated by General Zhukov's army, which bypassed Torun.

The Russians were advancing towards the Oder river but we were being taken well to the north and, having marched for twenty days, with only two rest days, we had reached the Baltic and the estuary of the river Oder by 7 February. Our eyes were henceforth fixed firmly to the West.

We were by now utterly exhausted. The blizzards, the lack of food and of warm shelter had taken their toll. We had spent most of the daylight trudging through the snow and the nights in whatever barn was available. One was wise, if one had enough strength left, to climb onto an upper floor. There were no toilets and in any case everybody was too exhausted to

---

[1] There was in fact considerable German resistance to General Rokossovsky's push towards the Baltic and the Russian penetration of Pomerania. Gdansk, Graudenz and Torun were stubbornly defended.

move. Those beneath sometimes found that the floor above leaked. At least one night was spent in the open. Several hundreds of us had been crammed and locked into an underground building (we were near to Peenemünde, where the VI rockets were developed). By one o'clock we were gasping for air. Fearing suffocation, we hammered on the doors in desperation and were thankful, when let out, to spend the rest of the night in the snow.

We spent the next few days crossing the estuary, across the low-lying and frozen islands of Wolin and Usedom. When we regained the mainland, on 10 February, the worst of the lame and sick left the column, some transportation having, at last, been found for them. Shortly afterwards a five-day halt was called. The only spare food was the potato – the land around produced little else. While the halt gave us a welcome rest, a diet of potatoes did little to restore our strength. On the first day of the halt, the guards carried out a search – it seemed a useless exercise, for we were down to virtually nothing. My diary did not interest them and the halt gave me the first opportunity of amplifying the brief notes which I was making at the end of every day's march.

16.2.1945: Diary

For the first time since the march began on January 20th, I've had sufficient time and mental recovery to write. I've a record of the route and daily distance. We've done according to my reckoning 500 kilometres, a daily average of 23 km per marching day. Each day has been very similar, none very easy. The difficulties have been manifold, increasing each day.

When, the first day, I decided not to stay, I knew I would probably regret it afterwards. I considered it a gamble with my life, and I expect quite a lot from life yet. The end is or seems to be near, so the stakes seemed too high.

We expected to go by rail; had we known it was to be such a march we may not have started. On the first stretch to Graudenz a lot of kit was jettisoned, even though some of the kit was being carried on a wagon. When we arrived in Graudenz camp and found that they had left marching and we were also to march, the place was littered with cases, boots, clothes, books, etc. We were given 4 days' rations, a loaf, a little sugar and about one and a half pounds bacon. I had some Red Cross and butter with me – food comprised half the weight of my pack. We departed the following morning. In the last quarter hour, Micky and I had made a sleigh out of a large-sized coal shuttle, which we named 'Hopeful'. It proved good value, especially after improvements to the runners, until just before Hammerstein [Stalag IIB]. A vital fitting broke when we were at the end of the column. Harassed and driven on by the merciless guards we just had to sling the packs on our backs.

We were fresh and in high spirits when we left Graudenz, the long line of sledges and cries of 'mush, mush' seems more of a sport but with each succeeding day the novelty faded. It took us a long time to cross the bridge. I was very disappointed when we did for I had hopes of being cut off by the rapidly advancing Russians. Later the hope revived when we heard that they had taken Bromberg [Bydgoszcz], but we never went via Stettin [Szczecin], but via Swinemünde.

The persistent hardship has been the uncertainty of the destination. The march has dragged on day after day, the guards themselves not knowing either. Even the evening's billet was often unknown. At first, it was the cold which worried us most and the lack of hot food and drink. The German captain in charge of the column I'm sure did his best, but usually it was a case of fending for oneself. Fortunately, we were allowed once or twice to build small fires. Micky and I managed fairly well. Sledging was made difficult by stretches of deep snow and the congested roads. The refugees were especially trouble-some, not only on the roads, but also as to finding a barn for the night. Very soon after setting out one morning someone told me my right ear was white. It had not seemed to me to be so cold nor did I feel anything. I had it rubbed until it bled and covered it with a dressing. At Hammerstein I had it dressed and it was rather badly frost bitten. Fortunately an ear is not one of the working parts.

Many thought Hammerstein the end but it was merely a day's rest. But a day's rest in comparative paradise for there was Red Cross ad lib. The American POWs were leaving also, so in order to empty the store each man could take what he could carry. A particular blessing was that each parcel contained 100 fags. Up to here, smokes had been very scarce. It was a day of feasting. From this point, 6 of us combined, I acting as QM. I gave each man pack-rations: 4 meats (3 lbs), 3 meat pastes (18 oz), one and a quarter lb chocolate, one quarter lb sugar, 10 oz coffee, half a pound of cheese and 400 fags. We built a strong sleigh which I named 'Confident'. Besides the packs it had to carry a large quantity of bread, biscuits, stews, jam and cheese. Moving out the following morning, we were in immediate difficulties for the load was too heavy. Fortunately I noticed a lovely model, about 7' x 4' with strong, thick runners. I think it was to carry the Jerries' kits for some lay near by. The situation called for desperate measures, so I took it in tow but hardly expected to get away with it. To catch up with the others, I covered it with kit and scattered in my haste many an Englishman and guard. And so we left Hammerstein; but not before we acquired a jug which has since proved invaluable. Since it was so heavy pulling the big sledge we put everything on it and abandoned 'Confident'. En route we had a lucky find of rope with which we made it possible for 6 to pull. These 3 days Micky was a passenger, his leg being swollen.

Unfortunately, after 3 days a rapid thaw made sleighing impossible, but for that period we had carried a heavy weight and also fed to capacity on good food.

From this point we came on pack rations and of course rationing. Instead of the cold and wet feet all and every day, food became the chief worry. All the Germans ever gave us was a very occasional bread issue, sometimes a little watery soup and an average of 1 lb per man of spuds per day. It wasn't so bad while our pack rations lasted (and our group lasted longer than most). We gradually became weaker and sickness was about 30–40%. Many were lame, some in fact had been sent away. But now many have dysentery, diarrhoea and sore feet.

It was hard indeed to resume marching on 20 February. We dragged our feet for another six days in a south-westerly direction, covering another 120 kilometres. When I next wrote up my diary, at the end of February, it was to report a steadily worsening situation.

27.2.1944: Diary

I am now writing on the 27th February. We've just had a thorough soaking – just another of the difficulties. I'm suffering from diarrhoea: in fact I've passed a little blood; but there's no medicine, no bandages, no ointments. If we hadn't sold a couple of watches and coffee we would be in a hopeless state.[1] As it is we are very weak. Rumours of Red Cross persist, there's supposed to be a dump made somewhere ahead but that may be just a jerry fairy-tale to keep us going. They have told us all sorts of lies on this march. Most of the guards have turned very nasty and although they know we're starving they prevent us dealing with civvies. They themselves will give a crust of bread for a tin of coffee and resell to civilians for a huge profit.

---

[1] That someone was still in possession of a watch surprises me.

It has been an endurance test. Firstly, the cold and snow; then sore feet; now lack of food, and sickness. Our stamina is gone. The pig swill we receive has very little nutrient and only causes sickness. Only Red Cross can save us from a serious catastrophe.

As we set out the next day, the British, French and Russians went separate ways. We were joined with another British column, and some of the men on it were from Stalag XXA. Fortunately, the rumour about Red Cross parcels proved correct. Although the distribution was only one parcel for every two men, it was a most welcome addition to the margarine, bread, sausage and sugar obtained by selling the watches and coffee. More relief came with an improvement in the weather. This allowed us to dry out. Then, on 3 March, we were cheered by our first sight of bombers, wave after wave clearly visible in the clear blue sky.

From there on, more days were spent at a halt than in marching. Obviously, the Germans had nothing better for us than the large barns into which several hundreds of us were herded. We were given a little dry food each day, and largely left to ourselves. The senior NCOs took charge, among them CMS Granger from Fort 13, and my services were soon in demand as interpreter. I was needed to help the sick receive treatment in a nearby town (Hagenow) and to help organise a makeshift wash-house. There was another desperately needed distribution of Red Cross food, this time three men to a parcel.

After having been halted for a whole week, we were suddenly marched 30 kilometres, only to be dumped for another week in buildings hardly any better from our point of view. However, in one respect our new abode turned out to be fortunate. The job of interpreter gave me the opportunity of making friendly contact with one of the farm workers, who not only invited me to share a meal with him but also allowed me to listen to the BBC news on his radio. With the volume turned down, I glued my ear to the set. I became a messenger bearing the good news that the Germans were everywhere in retreat. I

94

went the rounds, repeating it many times over in a low voice, with grim satisfaction.

On 19 March we were again on the move but those too sick to march had to be left behind. Among them was Tony Coulthard, who had helped in my escape from Fort 13. He was suffering from dysentery. He, like many others, lay in the straw too weak to move. There was nothing I could do to help him, except take him some food, a watery soup. He died on 24 March, one of the many unlucky ones to perish at the very end of our ordeal.

When we had nearly reached the Elbe, at Neuhaus about 50 kilometres from Hamburg, we began to follow the river upstream. I had the impression that we were heading into central Germany. Only when we crossed the river at Dömitz, did I feel reassured that we were still going in the right direction, towards the Allied troops advancing across the Rhine. We passed through Uelzen towards Celle. Beyond Celle lay Hanover.

I had not written up my diary for a whole month, apart from noting each day the distance covered, the weather and meals if any. I took advantage of a day's halt to write more fully.

26.3.45: Diary

Still marching. I've written very infrequently on this march. Firstly, because I shan't easily forget it and secondly each day's events and impressions are so very similar. Hunger is the chief problem; so far today I've not eaten and I've hunger pains in my stomach. The weather these last few days has been wonderful. Cloudless blue sky and a strong sun: in fact, I've been sun-bathing as soon as the day's march finished. Our destination is still uncertain: we are now on the Luneberger Heider [*sic*], about 30 km from Celle, but the popular rumour is that we are marching until April 4th. After we had had a fortnight's rest with only one day's march at the end of the first week to shift billets and change guards, we then finally moved off, leaving all sick behind. I felt more certain they had at last found somewhere to put us. Granger himself has been told by the Germans we are to be attached to a Stalag in this area. But another week's march will take us – where? Past Hanover. Still the uncertainty; it has been all along our greatest hardship. The best period for me was the second week of the fortnight's halt. I was acting as interpreter. That in itself was not remunerative but it gave me the freedom to form a friendship which once again gave me the comfort of a table, a chair, a plate and a full stomach. I was laid low for a day with the flu but made a speedy recovery. The route of the march this week took us up the Elbe to within 40 km of Ludwiglust, where we passed through three weeks previously.

Later that day, in late evening, we did get some bread, barley soup and potatoes. But we were also informed that a pig and some bacon had been stolen, and that we were all to be punished. My short diary entry at the end of the day was 'Day of rest and torture... Punishment on an empty stomach is a decider for me'. By that I meant that I would be looking for a good opportunity to escape. There was, however, no sign of punishment and our march simply continued the next day for another 18 kilometres. It took us to within 5 kilometres of Celle and the following morning we were taken into the town – to board a train. After more than two months and about 900 kilometres, the march seemed finally to have come to an end.

30.3.1945: Diary

At long last we are in a train. Tomorrow is Good Friday. In 1940 I spent Good Friday in a cattle truck going up to the Maginot line. It has been a horrible night – 60 to a truck. We saw extensive and intensive damage en route, especially at Hildesheim. Just before we entrained I saw Len Harvey and Basil Lambert – the first of the family I've seen. Sitting here in the cattle truck I notice around me 2 Bibles being read. The poor Bible, neglected whenever there is any other sort of entertainment, is nonetheless kept to the last, either because of religious instinct or because of its literary value, and is produced to be read at times like this.

My remarks about those reading the Bible show how little I understood. Had I been as familiar with the Bible then as I am now, I would have known why it was such a treasured possession. All of us were still clinging to life and wondering what lay ahead but those immersed in the Bible were tuned-in to the Easter message and the promise of eternal life.

The train, travelling in a south-westerly direction, took us to Hameln via Hildesheim then, returning in a north-easterly direction on another line towards Hanover. En route from Hameln, groups were dropped off at various places. I was in one of the two groups which left the train at Volgsen.

About 80 of us were crowded into a shed somewhere in the countryside. It was next to a limekiln and everything was covered in dust. I slipped out at the first opportunity to explore the neighbourhood. I came across some French civilian workers. They took me to their camp, which was unguarded, and I sat down with them for a most welcome meal. I was caught coming back, but the guard, mindful perhaps that it was Easter, or that he himself might soon be a prisoner, took no punitive action. I made two more visits over the Easter weekend, seeking food and information. I wanted to know where we were in relation to the front line. I knew that the Allies had managed to cross the Rhine but little of subsequent progress. It was nearly a fortnight since I had last listened to the BBC news.

On Easter Sunday I noticed that I too, like so many others, had been taken over by lice. We were reliving the early days of

1940 – once again undernourished, ragged and infested. I resumed the daily task of picking them out of my clothes and hair and crushing them between my thumbnails. But I was not thinking of the lice, nor of my ragged condition. I was concentrating on what might be in store for us. Why had we been transported by train to this place and provided with a regular daily ration: 230 grams of bread, 20 grams of margarine and a bowl of soup?

We could make a guess. We had seen the bomb damage the night we passed through Hildesheim. The fact that we had been split up and dropped off along the line of rail suggested that we were to be employed clearing up some of the mess. Hence, perhaps, the supply of food, for the Germans knew well enough that, if we were to be coaxed into doing some work, we had to be fed. But if our labour was to help the Germans militarily, food alone would not be enough. If some force was going to be used, only trouble lay ahead. Fortunately, the work did not start until the Wednesday after Easter and was cut short by the American advance. Just as in January we had been forced to march out of the reach of a Russian army, so now our guards were having to hurry us away from an American army advancing no less rapidly.

The encirclement of the Ruhr had been achieved at the beginning of April, and General Bradley's 12th Army Group was resuming its advance into Germany. General Simpson, commander of the 9th Army, no longer part of Montgomery's forces, had on 4 April received Bradley's orders, which concluded with the words 'be prepared to continue the advance on Berlin or to the north-east'.[1] Simpson and his men, happy no longer to be playing second fiddle in Montgomery's scheme of things to the north, had eyes only for Berlin. Unaware that Eisenhower was in fact planning to leave Berlin to the Russians, they raced ahead. German resistance was

[1] Charles B. MacDonald, *The US Army in World War II. The European Theater of Operations. The Last Offensive*, p. 382.

98

limited to 'isolated and small but bitter engagements'; the Americans were in effect 'striking into a vacuum'.[1]

We were thus right in the path of the 9th Army's advance. I had not been sent out with the others on the second day of work but had been sent into the nearby forest to collect wood for the kitchen. I was told how close we were to freedom when they returned. They had been in Hameln and had heard the sounds of battle. In the ensuing confusion several had managed to get away. The next day, Friday, 6 April, we remained in camp until the sudden order came to resume marching. By dusk we had travelled 16 kilometres and continued all next day for a further 30 kilometres, all in the wrong direction as far as we were concerned. It was obvious that there was nothing to be gained by delaying an escape any further. I had chosen to go west and I was not going to go east. The time had come for me to slip away and take my chance.

Two others, Steve and Joe, went with me. We were very hungry after the long march but calculated that the best moment to escape was as the evening's soup was being served, when the guards would probably be less vigilant. As we fled, some dogs barked but we got away safely. We kept going for a few miles, taking to the ditches whenever we heard footsteps or voices. On coming to a deserted shed, we decided to rest for the rest of the night, for we were quite exhausted. From information gained in the preceding week, I had drawn a rough map of the railways, roads and canals and we hoped that this would enable us to keep going in the right direction. We need not have worried for early next morning we spotted a French civilian. He and his wife had been working for the local Nazi party boss, who had already fled. It was suggested by the Frenchman, Ferdinand, that the house, now empty, would make a good hiding place for us. He put us in an attic room

---

[1] *Conquer: the Story of the Ninth Army 1944–45*, Washington, 1947, p. 291. MacDonald, p. 385, adds that 'Acres of rubble from Allied bombing and thousands of foreign laborers made overly exuberant by looted liquor posed more problems than did the Germans'.

and promised to bring us some food. We expected to remain hidden there for several days, but after a little more than 24 hours, there was a knock on the door. It was Ferdinand, accompanied by two American soldiers.

What joy, what luck. So fast had been the 9th Army's advance that it had already reached the River Leine. This was the line fixed by General Bradley for a coordinated advance by the whole 12th Army Group and General Simpson had been ordered to pause so as to allow the 1st and 3rd Armies to come abreast.[1]

It was this halt which had allowed Ferdinand to contact the Americans, men of the 701st Tank Battalion, and show them where he had hidden us.

A brief note in my diary that day began and ended with capital letters.

9.4.45: Diary

LIBERATED. It is almost incredible to realise we have been recaptured [sic] in such a short space of time. Just 48 hours ago we were POWs being forced to march eastwards out of the fighting zone. Now we are free. My emotions are so mixed, my thoughts so scattered. For several hours now I've been in conversation with American intelligence people about politics and Germans etc yet all the time I have been wanting to sit back and dream. Trying to behave normally while things are so abnormal. The comparison too vivid to absorb. Marching along on $1/_{12}$th of a loaf under guard – and now a grand meal and a feather bed – FREE.

The next two days seemed just as incredible. They were spent with a unit of the 102nd Division, the tanks of the 5th Armored Division having moved on. It was the 407th Infantry Regiment commanded by Colonel Wohner. He had encountered a few

---

[1] *Conquer: the Story of the Ninth Army*, p. 296.

days previously some stubborn German resistance 'in the heavily wooded Weser hills.[1]

Because of the casualties suffered, the half-trucks had some empty seats and Colonel Wohner invited us to take part in the mopping-up operations, while arrangements were being made for our evacuation. It was an irresistible opportunity. Even if I had been enrolled more as a spectator than as a combatant, and even if it was for only a few days, it could bear comparison with my brief and futile encounter with the German Army in Belgium, 1940. It was not all that shorter and it was infinitely sweeter to be able to help take Germans prisoner than to be taken prisoner by them.

There were other sights equally wondrous to someone whose experience was limited to the British Army of 1939–40. I could scarcely believe my eyes when it came to having a meal. We were virtually in the front line yet a cooked meal was served and, moreover, the officers queued with the men. I was even more amazed, a little later, when baseball kit was produced, and a game played. I was seeing a very different army from the one I had known. It was under proper command when in action but seemed otherwise oblivious of rank.

There was one sad note to my brief sojourn with the American troops – the death of President Roosevelt on 12 April. I observed how they were overwhelmed by grief when the news came through. I realised that he had been to them as much a leader as Churchill was to the people of Britain. He had obviously won their respect and their loyalty, and his death was felt as a personal loss.

Five days on from the day of our escape, I sat down to record something of what had been happening.

12.4.45: Diary

At last I've time and peace to write... It's difficult

---

[1] *Conquer: the Story of the Ninth Army*, p. 297.

to know where to start – in fact, I think I'll leave out details of escape and recapture. The biggest surprise last Monday was not being liberated: it was when I saw golden locks flowing out from underneath a tin hat: a girl in complete American kit. It was Suzy, a French girl who has travelled with the 5th Arm Div. doing 5th column work.

But that's just one of the surprises. Why did all three of us want to be captured by the Americans? I believe the other two, Steve and Joe, thought we would be better welcomed – in the usual lavish American manner. And I also, but in my case I believe there was a more subtle reason. Five years of this life and especially the last couple of months have made me so disgusted with my fellow Englishmen. Of course, I've only met the Americans under totally different circumstances; there will be, I suppose, 'hungry wolves' among them as well but I have only seen them as generous and hospitable fellows. I suppose it's for the same reason that now that I've been recaptured, I've no longer the urgent desire to see Blighty. Nevertheless, we've arranged not to go back with PWE,[1] but to join the 2nd British Army at Hameln, because we understand it will be a quicker route to Blighty. The home ties pull too strongly.

I should like to take home with me a good camera and watch, and so far I haven't been able to get hold of either... I never really thought of taking a camera or watch. Now, yesterday, we spoke to two Americans who had each a lovely camera and, from the conversation, they were out and out plunderers. Since then, I haven't had any peace of mind, I realize I've neglected the best opportunity to get what I want so badly, yet I know that I could never have plundered. In fact, at Sarstedt, I borrowed a lovely camera to take some photos and then returned it. Steve and Joe from the start have been

[1] Prisoner of War Evacuation – the way American POWs were to go.

collecting all sorts of things, many unnecessary, but I've been a restraining influence; but since they spoke to these two Americans they have been itching to plunder. On the other hand, the Jerries are sitting tight on what they have left. There has been a great deal of plundering by the Russians, Poles and Dutch, especially in Sarstedt where we spent Tuesday night. They were all walking about in new suits, boots and hats, yet I haven't a shirt even. I'm wearing just a pullover.

It was a queer sensation in Sarstedt. The tanks passed through and the military government is still behind, so that on Tuesday night there were no troops in the town. Had the Jerries known that they would have been underground. As it is, they keep all doors shut. One of the American MPs told me that there were about 10,000 Russians liberated who obtained arms and went about shooting up the Jerries and plundering. It required a whole company of MPs to control them. Another told me that he had seen a Russian chase a Jerry around a courtyard and finally club him.

I had a very interesting conversation with a S/Sgt the first evening immediately after recapture. We were being questioned by the officer who asked about how it was in *gefangenschaft*. We drifted onto various topics and he told me something about his job. It was part of intelligence and the handling of PWs. He seemed to know quite a bit of the psychological make up of a Jerry. It was, he said, very difficult for them to speak the truth. They have been told and have swallowed so many lies in the past that they think if they tell us a lie over and over again we will begin to believe it. There is however a method of obtaining the truth which has succeeded always. A Jerry is made to lie on the ground and told to lie motionless, otherwise he will be shot. A shot is fired. Those who are reluctant to tell the truth are nearby and hear the shot. They are then brought to view the body who is too scared to move an inch. Anyone, he said, who didn't then tell the truth was hard boiled. Most of the captured Wehrmacht were quite willing to disclose information even if it led to their friends being blown to bits.

My mind had flickered from one episode to another, like a butterfly. The result was this random account, out of sequence, seemingly disconnected. Yet there is a common thread. It is the question, what is and is not justifiable in the circumstances of war? I noted the methods used to obtain information about the enemy but refrained from comment. Presumably, those who are struggling desperately to defeat the enemy are permitted a trick or two. On the other hand, to deprive the defeated enemy of a camera or a watch is much more questionable. It is not quite clear whether I had stupidly missed the opportunity or had been restrained by conscience. Even Ferdinand's almost harmless outburst – he had turned on one of the German POWs and called him a *Schweinhund* – is mentioned and called into question.

My preoccupation with these instances of questionable behaviour has a paradoxical explanation, for it was something from which I had hoped to escape. Unacceptable conduct imposed on us, in 1940 and again on the march, was the reason I gave for wanting to be 'recaptured' by American rather than by British troops. New faces were to efface bad memories. It had not been sufficient to escape from the march, I also wanted to turn my back on that experience. The march had exposed us not only to blizzards, starvation and exhaustion but also to the almost inescapable necessity of putting one's own survival before the plight of others. The nearer anyone came to dropping out, the less hope there was of anyone stopping to help. One tended to grab whatever promised to keep one going. Otherwise, one simply risked being left behind, in the way that Tony Coulthard was left. It was, therefore, something of a shock to find myself still immersed in situations which allow, indeed require, man to decide, virtually unchallenged by others, what may or may not be done. I was recording the occasions which had revealed the need for deceit, the urge for revenge and the temptation to plunder. There was no escaping moral dilemmas.

I did not return home entirely empty-handed. I was invited to take my pick from a pile of discarded German weapons and equipment. I chose three trophies of war but they caused some embarrassment when I was back home. My sister did not want the German rifle in the house. The swastika pennant, which I attached to the car bonnet in celebration of VE day, a symbol of what had been conquered, only puzzled and angered those who saw it. The sword, complete with scabbard and tassel, lay in a drawer for some years before it too was discarded. I could have done better, one way or the other.

It was another week before I was finally on my way home. Colonel Wohner had been informed that British POWs were being evacuated from Bielefeld, so he sent me there. But, by the end of the next day, I was back in Hildesheim, only 2 kilometres from Sarstedt, my original point of departure. Someone in 2nd British Army had decided that Hildesheim should be the sole evacuation centre. The fruitless journey, the discomfort of travelling on the back of a lorry all day for two days, and the sheer waste of those two days, was hard to bear, especially when, on arrival at Hildesheim airfield, I saw that there was now a queue of many thousands, all waiting for a flight home. It was another three days before I took off. For the last time on German soil, I wrote in my diary.

17.4.45: Diary

A long wait. My name has finally been called. Plane 89. I'm not superstitious but Nancy once wrote [that] the number 9 is always, in numbers and dates, associated with me. Captured May 19. Court-martialled January 19th. Liberated April 9th. Plane 89. I feel a lot better now I've a place. I'll probably go tomorrow, perhaps today.

It was to be the morrow, and because of an overnight stopover in Brussels, I landed in Britain only on Thursday, the 19th. Another 9. I was in fact arriving home well in advance of many others. There had been numerous columns of POWs from Stalags XXA and XXB marching out of northern Poland and across northern Germany that winter. Some of these seemed to have made slower progress than ours and to have been turned around while still east of the Elbe river. Like us, they had been put to work repairing bomb damage to the railways, their lives at risk every day. Some ended up as far north as Lübeck, on the Baltic coast, and were not liberated until early May.

I even arrived home at much the same time as those liberated at the end of January by Russian troops between Torun and Bydgoszcz. Those liberated by the Russians may have been spared the march but even so they found themselves trapped in Poland. They were kept there because Stalin was waging a political as well as a military campaign – the extension westwards of communist influence, an objective which Churchill and Roosevelt sought to frustrate. They had reluctantly conceded at the Teheran Conference in November 1943 that the frontiers of Poland would have to be redrawn to take account of the annexation of eastern Poland, which had been occupied by Stalin's troops, by agreement with Hitler, when Poland was attacked in 1939. Still to be settled, however, were two thorny issues; the siting of a new Polish-German frontier and the formation of a new Polish government. When the three leaders next met, in February 1945 at Yalta, the first issue was left partly in obeyance. The other issue, who could legitimately speak for Poland, was apparently resolved by Stalin's assurance, first, that any provisional Polish government would include representatives of both sides, the Polish leaders located in London and those located in Russia, and secondly, that in due course the Poles would be free to elect their own government. But there could be no free elections if power had already been seized by Stalin's protégés.

This was Stalin's objective and the POWs were caught up in it. His determination to achieve a fait accompli meant the elimination of any potential Polish opposition. Consequently, the pace of the Red Army's advance through Poland was dictated as much by political as by military considerations. It was necessary after each offensive for the Red Army to pause, not only in order to regroup but also so that it could be an army of occupation. The most flagrant demonstration of this policy was the way the Germans were given a free hand to repress the Warsaw uprising in August 1944. The Polish Home Army, watched by Russian forces close to hand, bled to death. Likewise, Polish partisans, who had assisted the Russian advance by harrying the retreating Germans, had to be neutralised, and everywhere the population intimidated into accepting a communist regime. This took time.[1]

For the Allied POWs liberated by the Russians, there was no question of a speedy repatriation. The Russians, preoccupied with their own objectives, kept them under guard, in conditions little or no better than when they were in German hands. Some found themselves arrested, interrogated and imprisoned. Anyone who could not convince the Russians of his identity was suspect and held for investigation.[2]

The Allied POWs had in fact become pawns, used by Stalin in his struggle for hegemony in Poland. There had been an agreement, signed by Russian, British and American representatives in Moscow on 11 February, which set out arrangements for the repatriation of POWs. It was supposed to be a reciprocal agreement whereby each was to be given speedy access to their own nationals and given charge of their repatriation. It was to prove, recorded General Deane, the

---

[1] Stalin was in fact faced with a dilemma. '... there was little hope of assuaging Polish hostility without a clear commitment to the country's freedom and hence to the return of the Polish government from London. In that case, all ambitions for a 'socialist Poland' would have to be abandoned. In other words, if Stalin were to press on for Berlin without first solving the Polish conundrum, he would be courting military disaster. Yet if he were to safeguard the Red Army by making concessions to the Poles, he was risking political failure. From the Kremlin's viewpoint, the most satisfactory solution was for all independent Polish forces to be eliminated before the decisive battle for Berlin was joined.' Norman Davies, *The Soviet Occupation of Poland 1944–45*, in *The end of the War in Europe 1945*, ed. Gill Bennett, HMSO, 1996.
[2] See Nigel Cawthorne, *The Iron Cage*, 1992. Detailed accounts of what some POWs had to endure are to be found in official files, in diaries deposited with the Imperial War Museum, in Scotty Young, *Descent Into Danger*, 1954, and in W. R. Alderson, *The Long Road Back*, 1994.

American representative, 'just another piece of paper', no better than the agreement to hold free elections.[1]

The Allies were never given any information as to the numbers and whereabouts of their POWs. No American or British representatives were allowed into Poland until 1 March, and even then, they were restricted in their movements. All attempts to contact the POWs were blocked with the assertion that they were already on their way to Odessa, the sole place designated by the Russians for the handover. This assertion was manifestly a lie; Poland had simply been declared out of bounds to the Allies. They were not to have the opportunity of seeing for themselves what was happening to the Poles. Moreover, repatriation was being delayed as a tactic – to force Roosevelt and Churchill to concede Stalin's two demands: recognition of his protégés as the rightful Provisional Government of Poland, and the repatriation of Russians held by the Allies in the west, some of whom had put on German uniforms. The Russian authorities wanted these segregated and handed over. With great reluctance the Allies complied with the first demand and went some way towards meeting the demand to hand over men who would almost certainly be put to death. Not to have done so could possibly have jeopardised the safe return of the Allied POWs in Russian hands.

Thus it was that, throughout February and March, Stalin, Churchill and Roosevelt were engaged in a verbal tussle, in an exchange of telegrams progressively sharper in tone. It merely gave Stalin the time he needed to consolidate his hold on Poland and it demonstrated the truth of the adage that possession is nine-tenths of the law. Moreover, as Nigel Cawthorne has so pertinently remarked, 'The Soviets, complete masters of the game, were blackmailing the West with something they said they didn't have' – tens of thousands of Allied POWs.

While these diplomatic exchanges were taking place, the

---

[1] John R. Deane, *The Strange Alliance*, Viking Press, 1947, p. 189.

POWs themselves were being told by their 'liberators' that they were being guarded for their own safety – a statement not exactly untrue, for Poland was a very unsafe place for anyone seeking to evade authority. Safety implied patience and acceptance of the assurance that everyone would be repatriated 'as soon as transport is available'.

Naturally, not everybody was prepared to sit and wait. Three American officers must have been quick off the mark, for they reached the American Mission in Moscow on 17 February. It helped if one was still in possession of some coffee or chocolate, commodities which had been used to bribe German guards and which were now used to obtain shelter and transportation in a bid to find one's own way home. It was nearly March before the Russians began to move the POWs to Odessa for embarkation. Only in April did they set foot on British soil.

Once back home, it no longer mattered how one had arrived. When I got in touch with Tony Coulthard's family it was to be told that he had not survived. Nor had many others. The number of British POWs who did not survive the march across Germany or who failed to return via Russia might be recorded somewhere but not that of the Russians POWs. Life was cheap in those closing weeks of the war. Jews, Poles and Russians, too weak to join in an evacuation, were slaughtered in their thousands. High-ranking Germans imprisoned on suspicion of having been privy to or sympathetic to the attempt on Hitler's life in July, 1944 were taken out and executed. So were those, some of them British, who had been caught while engaged in undercover operations behind German lines.

Perhaps the unluckiest of all were the British POWs whose plane blew up en route to England and the three Americans killed in Odessa by a falling wall.[1]

---

[1] The information about other columns and various fatalities has been obtained from accounts and diaries deposited in The Imperial War Museum, London.

9

Starting Afresh

We flew home from Brussels in a Stirling on a clear day. From the second pilot's seat, I had a wonderful view of land and sea. (Was there no second pilot? Or was the seat kindly offered to me for a short while?)

What a joy it was to be back in England. My telephone call home brought the long-awaited news that I was safe. Two days later I arrived home on six weeks' leave.

2.5.45: Diary

Homecoming was grand. It's all indelibly recorded in my memory so there is no need to write about it. The flags flying in the Orchard were an embarrassing shock, so were all the neighbours who rushed out to shake hands. But they are all so kind – and one even sent a jar of chicken breasts to help me recuperate and I arrived home looking extremely fit.

Father gave me a watch. I was really lost without one. I'm beginning to feel a little tired now, but I find myself refreshed after 6 or 7 hours.

Physical recuperation was not the major problem. Ex-POWs were accorded double the standard civilian ration of food and I experienced nothing worse than a mild bout of jaundice. More problematical was the process of reintegration, with my family, the army and society in general. There was a five-year gap to be bridged which was more than a simple lapse of time. Self-isolation, the answer to unwelcome aspects of life while a POW, had become an ingrained reaction which now stood in the way of a free and easy adjustment to new surroundings. However familiar these might appear to be, they were in fact full of novelty and surprise. I am reminded of my reactions by what I recorded at the time – in a newspaper article, in a poem and in my diary. I experienced not only joy but also bewilderment and dismay.

Acting on my resolution to earn some money by writing, I submitted an article to the *Manchester Guardian*, which appeared on 15 May 1945. It told of my encounter with the American troops and mentioned some of the surprises and difficulties which awaited me on reaching home. I wrote:

For a whole week I was amazed to hear English spoken in the streets. I am so used to a background of German. The first days were full of shocks to the senses – the brilliance of white bread fascinates me – the heat of an English open fire is unbearable – the sudden shattering noise of the telephone startles me – the Union Jack, and flowers on a white tablecloth, the tick of a grandfather clock, and the dark green of spring cabbage, tasting so different from the savoys we had in Germany, are all surprises.

There are several difficulties accompanying a sudden release from imprisonment: above all, a returning sense of responsibility and obligation. For five years, I have been under forced restraint, under enemy orders. To disobey, to rebel, was a duty and often a necessity. Now I cannot suddenly assume voluntary restraint: it must be gradual and it is difficult. Similarly, I've had for five years my day's activities arranged for me. Time had meant little to me. Now I have the freedom to choose – to walk if I so wish – or to turn on the radio – or to go to see someone. Sudden freedom of choice is like an intoxicating drink and here also I must learn self-restraint Slowly

111

the clock and personal relationships are beginning to control my life once more. Old friends understand and are tolerant, but still I cannot meet new people and make polite conversation.

Readjustment to normal life – to the clock and others around me – had its sometimes comic, sometimes distressful, moments. One such was a visit to my sister-in-law, who had prepared the traditional high tea, using up precious rations. I could not face it and told her that all I wanted was a crust of bread. On another occasion I got up in the middle of the night feeling hungry. In the larder I found a plate of food, all prepared, which I ate. I was told next morning that I had deprived the dog of its breakfast. My failure one day to keep an appointment with my father was much more distressing. We had arranged a rare outing together, a visit to the cinema. I was probably thinking of this lamentable lapse of memory when writing the final paragraph of my article.

Poetry, rather than prose, was the more appropriate medium for expressing my unbounded sense of freedom. So intense, so ecstatic was my joy that I felt like a lark, soaring above everything. I was free not only of constraints imposed by captivity. I was breathing an air that freed me from the cares of the world. I did not need any drug to produce this sense of total freedom, of boundless energy. I was simply living in the moment, for the moment, without constraints of any kind, physical or moral, accepting both joy and sadness in equal measure. My values were aesthetic and hedonistic. Beauty and harmony were more important than morals.

> Down on that earth, where lies my hidden nest
> Lives mortal man who, though of other tongue
> And different shape, is by Nature blessed
> Like me, in want of food, love and rest.
> Yet only sorrow echoes my joyful song.
>
> When at dusk I descend to sleep
> He often disturbs my slumbers deep
> With noisy car and blinding light.

But at the dawn when I impatient soar
To meet the sun, a ball of crimson gore
He sleeps on as if still night.

I sing my praises and hover in the sky
To drop and take an unsuspecting fly
But he, midst blackening smoke and deafening noise
Seeks not food but seeks catastrophe
He notices not his growing atrophy
To life's beauty: he knows not my joy.

The magic joy of spring, when I sing so lightly
And in winged flight pursue my season's fancy
He knows, yet distinguishing right and wrong
He cloaks his love in artificial sanctity.
For love alone is judge, not morality,
Whether we love in sorrow or in song.

I was brought down to earth when my leave finished. Once back in barracks I faced having to make the hardest readjustment of all. That the clock and family obligations should reimpose themselves was understandable and acceptable. To have the army once more regimenting my life was much less so but unavoidable. The war with Japan was not yet over and I had to be retrained. I felt as if everything had been rewound back to 1939. Although the weapons were different – I was being introduced to the Sten gun – and the accommodation much superior, the army of 1945 seemed otherwise not to have changed. This time it was, in fact, even worse, for I was back at the bottom of the pile, without the compensation of having my friends from Wallasey for company. I felt trapped and thought that, unless I found some means of escape, I was going to be very frustrated and unhappy. For a while it was indeed the case. My reactions, recorded in my diary, show how disgruntled I was feeling.

15.6.1945: Diary

The MO ... has given me 14 days' light duty, which excuses me such obnoxious activities as PT and playing soldiers too heartily. The Army has made me laugh and cry to-day. This morning, an address by the CO and then two films, *Civil Defence* and *Liberation of Rome* – all guns and bangs. We were then presented with all sorts of things but no instructions. We were left to our own devices to sort out ... the pack, the gas cape, the straps, the groundsheet etc and to piece it all together. I watched the others who seemed to know how and copied. This afternoon there was an intelligence test for personnel selection. English, e.g. spell CAT. Arithmetic, $2+3 = ?$ They seem to realise like I do the appalling ignorance and stupidity of many Britons. But what shocked me was an algebra and trig paper. Full of sine, cosine, logs, areas of triangles, etc. A lot of it beat me ...

16.6.1945: Diary

Today we had an observation test. Visited Aylesbury. Dinner at the Bull's Head. Officers, civilians stared at me: a private! Tut! Tut! All leave, I have been in civvies in far more exclusive places and been accepted, in fact welcomed. It's sickening to think that I did 8 months, at the beginning of the war, to become not an officer but a POW, and now, I've got to do 12 months to become a civilian. You expected one dose of it to become an officer. To have a second dose in order to get a release on time, stay in the ranks to the bitter end, is galling.

Fortunately, things did not turn out so badly. I was rescued, presumably, by a better than average performance in the intelligence test and by the requirement that the army should provide some basic education in current affairs. In early July I was asked to give a lecture and later that month was sent to

Cambridge on a two-week course. That was heaven indeed. I punted all the way to Granchester and swam in Byron's pool.

However, the army took its time in deciding what to do with me. I found myself shunted around – first Blackpool, then Helmsley, and then Skipton. I was even put on a draft for the Middle East. Finally, in December, I was transferred to the Army Educational Corps and given the rank of sergeant. Posted to Scotland, I roamed the hills and enjoyed the wild open spaces.

Meanwhile, my own dreams were taking shape. I told my father of my plans to go to university and of how I hoped to finance myself. He generously offered to help but he must have had reservations, especially about my interest in philosophy. No member of the family had ever attended a university. Nor did my friends comprehend. I had not made much progress writing the novel but I was still optimistic. The *Manchester Guardian* had paid me three guineas for my article and it had been reproduced by the Ministry of Information. I was discovering, however, that writing a novel is a difficult art, especially when one is at the beck and call of the army.

I had more success in securing a place at university. I had my eye on Cambridge, having been enchanted by my two weeks there in the summer. I consulted the headmaster of Wallasey Grammar School – still F. L. Allan – who arranged for me to meet the Senior Tutor of Emmanuel College, Mr Welbourne. I was rather discouraged when he told me that the kind of philosophy which interested me had ceased to thrive in Cambridge. It was being taught to fewer than 25 undergraduates, for whom it was only a subsidiary subject. Philosophy per se was in the hands of a Professor Wittgenstein, an iconoclast according to Welbourne, but, as I discovered later, an influential one. Welbourne suggested that I was more likely to find what I wanted in Oxford rather than Cambridge.

Disappointed, I turned once again to Allan, who recommended Merton College. But no assurance of a place there was forthcoming, not even provisionally. I was told that the college was waiting to see how many ex-servicemen would be returning to resume their studies. I was, however, told that Keble

College might have a vacancy for someone like me and my spirits rose on learning from Keble that I could be considered. I would have to sit an entrance examination and this would not be held until March 1946. For the next three months I was in suspense, all my hopes pinned on Keble. I was lucky. The College found room for me and in the following October my new life began.

POSTSCRIPT

This postscript has a double purpose. It tells first of discovering, from a visit to Belgium in 1990, how the villagers of Isières had buried our dead and recorded the 'battle' which took place on 19 May 1940. Secondly, it provides a sequel for readers who might like to know both how I came to view the war, and what became of doubting Thomas, that is to say, my refusal to accept Christian answers to questions raised in 1944.

May 1940 Revisited

Like many others who had been with the BEF, the Marshall brothers and I wished to commemorate the fiftieth anniversary by retracing our steps. We planned a quiet private visit, free of crowds and officialdom, but discovered that Isières had planned something quite different. Unbeknown to us, the events of 19 May 1940 had entered into local history in ways we never could have imagined. First and foremost, some brave and compassionate persons had ventured out to collect the bodies of those killed. These were taken to the local cemetery for burial. They lay there in an unmarked grave, tended by the local schoolchildren, until the Liberation, when the local schoolmaster, François Delhove, launched a public subscription so that a memorial stone could be erected. It lists the names of the nine who were killed, eight 4th Cheshires and one from the Oxfordshire and Buckinghamshire Light Infantry. Heading the list is not Captain Lucking but Major Williams, a confusion caused by the fact that one of Lieutenant Williams' forenames was Major. The village of Isières had thus adopted our dead and cared for them until the War Graves Commission took charge of the grave and erected nine individual crosses. Unfortunately, these were placed in front of the memorial stone, almost obscuring it. Happily changes have been made as a result of our visit. Representations were made, through the regiment, to the commission, and the nine crosses, which did not mark individual graves, have been realigned, allowing the memorial stone to be seen unimpeded.

In addition, two of the local inhabitants had taken it upon themselves to record the so-called 'battle of the river Dendre' in the form of a diorama. It is on a massive scale, measuring about 15 metres long and 3 metres wide. The information available to those who made it was unfortunately too scanty for it to provide a full and proper picture of what actually took place but, used over the years as a teaching aid in the local school, it has helped to make 19 May a date to remember. Kept in store because of its size, it is brought out at appropriate times, almost a local icon.

The discovery that Isières, in consultation with the regiment, was preparing some kind of official commemoration left the three of us wondering whether our own idea of a low-key remembrance had not been jeopardised. But on the day all our reservations were swept aside both by the intimacy of the occasion, focused as it was on our fallen comrades whom we had known so well, and also by the warmth of the welcome shown to us survivors.

The day began with Mass in the village church. Belgian ex-servicemen had placed themselves around the altar. The priest consecrating the bread and wine was almost lost from sight when they lowered their colours over the altar. It was, for me, an intrusion on the sanctity of the Mass, on a par with the German Army's motto 'Gott mit uns'. I was heartened by the priest's sermon, for he did not mince his words about the

118

need to forgive and about the iniquity of perpetuating old quarrels.

From the church we went in procession to the cemetery. Colonel Wild of the Cheshire Regiment, from the nearby NATO Headquarters, led our homage. Also present were three former officers of the 4th Battalion, James McGuinness, Geoffery Clemence and Cecil Anderson. They had come to convey to the village, and especially to the Delhove family, the regiment's appreciation and they were also on their way to visiting all the known 1940 Cheshire graves. For each grave, they had brought a small wooden cross. We placed our wreaths, including one on François Delhove's grave, and in silence spanned the years.

Later in the day, we searched for places we could recognise. Various parts of the village and surrounding areas, those which the diorama depicted as having been the scene of some action, had been staked out and signposted but none of these corresponded to anything we remembered. Eventually, we were able, with some local help, to locate the farmyard where the platoon's trucks had been parked and the road where we were ambushed.

After Isières we made for Cassel, where Norman Marshall had been taken prisoner. En route, we passed close to Enghien, a name Norman recognised. He had been wounded and his left arm had been amputated. For several weeks he had been held in a building from which he could see a signpost to Enghien. It so happened that the proprietor of the garage where we stopped for petrol, when told Norman's story, brought out a collection of old picture postcards. One of these was of a nearby convent school, the very place in question. The sisters were very happy to show Norman around.

As we approached Cassel we could easily visualise its importance in 1940. From the hilltop, it commands several road junctions. Our battalion, already much reduced in strength – A and C Companies had been amalgamated after the withdrawal from the river Dendre – had stood fast in Cassel for five days, until, surrounded, the order was given 'every man for himself'. Norman easily recognised the building where his gun had been positioned and was even able to locate the spot where, trying to make his way out, he was wounded and taken prisoner. Our success, at both Isières and Cassel, in retracing our steps added to our feeling that the trip had been well worth while. For some weeks thereafter it dominated our minds.

We did not join the crowds gathering at Dunkirk for the official ceremonies on 26–27 May. Instead we went to Wormhoudt, a small town on the road from Cassel to Dunkirk. There, on 28 May 1940, men of the SS Leibstandarte Adolf Hitler Regiment had taken about 100 prisoners and later in the day had massacred them. Nearly all the prisoners had been stripped of their identity discs and private possessions. They were herded into a small barn and callously butchered. They were mostly men of the 2nd Royal Warwickshire Regiment but some were of our own 4th Battalion – 8 Platoon of B Company and 15 Platoon of D Company. Miraculously, there were about a dozen survivors, who later were able to make known what had happened. Nearly all those killed lie in graves marked 'unknown', a reminder of how horrible and how random war can be.

Almost as random has been the process of bringing to justice those responsible for this and other war crimes. Near Wormhoudt, at Le Paradis, about the same number of prisoners, men of the Royal Norfolk Regiment, had been massacred the previous day by men of the SS Totenkopf Regiment. The British War Crimes Interrogation Unit was able to establish that the officer who gave the order at Le Paradis was Fritz Knoechlein. He was tried, convicted and hanged. This Interrogation Unit was, however, disbanded before it could complete its investigations into the Wormhoudt massacre. It was never able to question Wilhelm Mohnke, the officer strongly suspected of having given the order. He was with Hitler in Berlin at the end of the war and was captured by the Russians. He was not released for many years and has never been brought to trial, despite the overwhelming nature of the evidence against him.[1]

[1] The case against Mohnke is set out by Ian Sayer and Douglas Botting in *Hitler's Last General*, Bantam Press, 1989.

The futility of war

Although thankful in 1945 that the war in Europe had ended with the defeat of Hitler, I had difficulty in reconciling myself to the end result in Eastern Europe. My thoughts were often with the Poles. They had fought the war as one of the Allies but had been cheated of victory. Freed from Hitler, they were now enslaved by Stalin. I could not gloss over this fact when reflecting on the war, its purposes, its horrors and its results. My own debt to the Poles was too great for that. I also knew, all too clearly, what was happening in Poland. I knew it from POWs who had come home via Russia. Held up for many weeks in Poland, they had witnessed the Russian-backed takeover. I knew about it also from the Poles I had met when home on leave. I met them at Poulton Hall, the home of Mrs Lancelot Green, a champion of their cause. I felt it necessary to speak out but when I did so, at a meeting of the Wallasey Rotary Club, what I had to say did not go down very well. Russia was the great ally immune from criticism. After all, what could be done about it? It was a question I had asked myself. With heavy heart, I had written in my diary:

I don't want to think about it. Everything will turn out all right. Isn't six years of war enough? Aren't you sick of it?

Yes, I am sick. There's a horrible feeling in the bottom of my stomach. The world has grown evil – horribly evil. We've beaten the Germans and hanged their leaders. We fought for freedom and decency and we've won. Now let's get back to a bit of decent living...

On getting back to England and hearing about the concentration camps I realised that Germany had waged war in a brutal fashion and with set purpose. I fortunately hadn't met the worst Germans but had learnt enough about them to know that these stories were true, whereas people in this country seemed a little incredulous and

121

found it hard to imagine that any human being could be so inhuman... At last I felt glad we had gone to war...

Then I began to think of how we were going to prevent it ever showing its face again. But that only lasted a minute. To my horror I saw that Naziism was not beaten. It still existed, on the side of the triumphant allies, under the name of Bolshevism. My friends came out of Germany via Russia. I spoke to Poles who escaped from Russia. I remembered Katyn, where the Russians murdered and buried thousands of the Polish officers. I remembered how the Russian army stopped in front of Warsaw and let the Germans kill off what was left of the Polish Nationalists ... how England had to send planes 600 miles to Warsaw when the Russians were only 20 miles away. And I realised that, having found justification for the war against Germany, I had found justification for a war against Russia. It would be purely farcical to stop half-way, like trying to get rid of rabbits in the UK by killing them off in England but leaving them alone in Wales. Yet who wants to go to war; that is what makes me sick. I want to live in peace: but then I vomit at the thought of being hypocritical. Either war with Germany was justified, and if that is so, so is war with Russia justified. But there is really no alternative: no one can believe in Naziism or that the war with Germany was a mistake. Are we therefore to go to war against Russia?

No ... the Russians are ignorant, callous, cruel, used to slavery and hard toil ... as anyone who has seen them will testify. So I am willing to let Stalin experiment; he is not so much worse than the Czar...

But what about Poland, Yugoslavia, Romania, Bulgaria? I don't know much about the last three ... take Poland as an example. We know the Poles are intensely national-istic and patriotic. We know they don't like the Russians any more than they like the Germans. But the weak must respect the strong; it seems Russia wants Eastern Poland ... you can't beat your head against a brick wall. The important thing is to accept the new proposed frontiers, get the Big Four to guarantee them and then to start to build the new Poland. It is the only chance. As she feels her feet, the internal situation will improve. I know a Russian controlled government is in power, that those who oppose are interned and disappear without trial. But are there so many Russian admirers in the Polish ranks? Are they not a nation which has resisted Russia and Germany; do these traditions die with those who were killed at Katyn and at Warsaw?... The thought of playing ball with the Russians even for the next ten or twenty years is nauseating; but what is the alternative?... Nothing is perfect and often the second best has to be tolerated... Life doesn't give you all you want.

Now that the Cold War has also ended, after no less than half a century, we are confronted anew with the old problem of how to secure peace among the nation-states of Europe. Twice within this present century, their frontiers have been reshaped by war, drastically so in Central and Eastern Europe. Let us recall what happened. Hitler took over Austria and parts of Czechoslovakia. He and Stalin secretly agreed to partition Poland. Stalin took the opportunity to incorporate the Baltic states of Estonia, Lithuania and Estonia into the Soviet Union. Poland, having had its eastern borders amputated by Stalin in 1939, was compensated at the expense of Hitler's Germany. East Prussia (except for around Königsberg, which Stalin retained and renamed Kaliningrad) and all the land east of the river Oder and of the western branch of the river Neisse became part of Poland.[1] This drastic reshaping of the map was accompanied by a massive resettlement of Poles and Germans. Over 8 million Germans fled from or were driven out of their homelands. Millions of Poles moved westwards. It was ethnic

---

[1] Churchill and Roosevelt had tried at the Potsdam Conference to fix the frontier on the eastern branch of the Neisse. Agreement was deferred until the signing of a peace treaty, which never took place.

cleansing, as it is now called, on a grand scale. What was left of Germany became a nation divided into East and West.

The subsequent disintegration of the Soviet Union and of Yugoslavia has called the map of Europe once more into question and, in the case of Yugoslavia, we are again witnessing one of Europe's periodic fits of madness. When and how will we Europeans manage to outlaw these futile attempts to settle our disputes by means of war?

There is some hope. NATO is being extended, albeit with Russian objections, to bring some of the East European countries under its umbrella. Membership of the European Union may be expanded without any loss of the cohesion which has already been achieved. Indeed, it is widely accepted, at least on the continent of Europe, if not in the United Kingdom, that it is urgent to move towards a more united Europe. Although a united Europe – even one which is united in an irrevocably binding fashion – will not remove all frictions of a nationalist nature, it would require them to be resolved by means short of war. There would be little chance of another Hitler or Mussolini. Moreover, a strong united Europe need not fear an attack from without. Might it not be wise to seize the chance, while the experience of war, and of all that it can entail, is still within living memory, to banish from Europe this barbaric scourge of war? We owe some sacrifice of national sovereignty to those who were sacrificed in two world wars.

Doubting Thomas

When, in 1944, I began to question myself as to where and how I stood, morally and spiritually, and when in October 1946 I turned to Oxford for help, I was beginning a journey which has proved never-ending. I found the answers not in books but in a series of personal encounters. The first of these occurred in my second term at Oxford. Bishop Neill, who was leading an Anglican mission to the university, delivered an address on 'Sins, Ancient and Modern'. This sounded interesting. I was so impressed by his address that I immediately returned to my rooms and recorded it in my diary.

> Firstly, he is ... an orator of the highest order. Rarely, in fact never before, have I heard a clock tick during a pause in a speech, not in a place the size of the Sheldonian. And I was sitting far from the clock.
>
> Secondly, he presented his subject – Sins, Ancient and Modern – intelligently, authoritatively, yet as an argument, i.e. he appealed to our reason not to our faith, most obviously sincerely, cogently and also with moments of wit and telling antithesis.
>
> ... I, a non-Christian, a disbeliever ... was impressed by his arguments ... especially by their possible truth ... even to the extent of feeling what a fearsome fate is God's displeasure.
>
> In a parenthesis, he dealt with sexual intercourse and chastity. He did not consider this such a great sin as cruelty, avarice and malice. Yet in the last few months he had become convinced the Church was right... In sexual matters what is right is self-control, both before and after marriage: this admits of no exception, neither in time, place, circumstances, nor for any person, man or woman...
>
> Sin was an error. Instincts are all good, including the sex instinct... But sin is error in time, place and measure. In place, when we are promiscuous. In measure, when we abuse it. Sexual intercourse is creative and should only be used for creative purposes...

I ended with the sentence: 'I've more to say but I have to write an essay on Kant's Metaphysical Deduction of the Categories'. A rather different subject. A better subject for that night's essay would have been Kant's Categorical Imperative.

I wonder how many of today's Anglican bishops would so capture a student audience? One who would speak like Bishop Neill, if there be such a one? Certainly not those who appear to be at sixes and sevens on questions of right and wrong behaviour.

The second encounter, a few months later, pointed me in the same direction but involved a more definite response. I met the girl I wanted to marry who happened to be a French Catholic. We met as students in the summer of 1947, not at Oxford but in Goettingen. We had both been selected to spend a few weeks there, in the summer of 1947, with some German students. We were participants in a scheme to break down the isolation which the German universities had suffered during the Nazi regime. At the time, Allied personnel occupying Germany were enjoined not to fraternise with any of the defeated enemy. To be exempted from this general rule was an odd experience. We, the visitors, were each paired off with one of the German students to live as one of the family. Our hosts had very little food to offer and they much appreciated the more substantial rations which were allocated to us as Allied personnel. Our fraternisation was not limited to the home and the university campus. We spent the evenings drinking in the local taverns. When we ventured to observe the controversial student practice of dancing round and kissing the statue of the Gänzeliesel – the legendary goose-girl; controversial because the local authorities had once outlawed such frivolity – the police looked on, not sure what to do.

I have to admit that I neglected my duties by preferring to fraternise with one of the French students. I accompanied her back home to meet her parents. I found myself back in Lorraine, where I had spent the early spring of 1940. They were not a little surprised but I think I made a good impression. My visit followed that of an English girl who, well-mannered in the English fashion, had eaten daintily and refrained from commenting on the food she had eaten. I, hungry after three weeks of short rations, ate with gusto and left no doubt that I had enjoyed my meal.

When it came to the question of marriage, at the end of 1948, I had to make up my mind. I was about to marry into a Catholic family but what was I? I was not sure. I had, following Bishop Neill's address, tentatively gone down on my knees, not praying so much as seeking some assurance of God's existence. I was still far short of being a firm believer. I had not much time to make up my mind. A new British Nationality Act was due to come into force. My fiancée – actually we were not even officially engaged – was training to be a lawyer and had no wish to renounce her French nationality. There was no need to do so if we married before the end of the year.

I decided to step the whole way, from tentative belief to communion with the Catholic church. The parish priest, a long-standing friend of the family, was given no time to instruct me in the faith. He took me on trust and gave me his blessing, after I had answered satisfactorily at least the final question, uttered I think in some desperation, 'Well, you do believe in Jesus Christ?' What I know of the faith has been learnt subsequently, in attending Mass and through a third encounter.

This took place nearly ten years later and in a roundabout way. My wife had written a thesis on Gandhi for her doctorate of law.[1] She was helped in its publication by Lanza del Vasto. He had lived for a short while with Gandhi, and had subsequently gathered together, in his Communauté de l'Arche, a small following of his own. One of them was Jacques Goettman, a priest known as 'Petit Père', for he was little more than 5 feet in height. It was he who made me a confirmed believer. He taught me a way to understand the Bible that I found both convincing and inspiring. I joined the reading parties which he organised each summer. We camped high in the Alps for several weeks, well above the tourist line. He concentrated his wonderful power of exegesis on the book of Genesis and on the message of Jesus as told by St John. Becoming more and more immersed in the faith each summer, I compared myself to the Easter candle which is thrice lowered into the baptismal water, each time more deeply. At the

---

[1] *Gandhi Contre Machiavel*, deNoel, 1963; English edition *Gandhi Against Machiavellism: Non-Violence in Politics*, Asia Publishing House, 1966.

summer camp of 1965, Petit Père arranged for me to receive the sacrament of confirmation.

It may be contended that, in 1948, the cart had been put before the horse, that the doors of the church should not have been opened to me while doubts remained about my beliefs. I admitted once, to a colleague at LSE, that I had to some extent acted out of prudence rather than conviction. My marriage was going to be a mixed one, of language, culture and nationality. It would help if my wife and I were at least to share the same creed. My colleague, Ralph Miliband, a true Marxist, was shocked by what appeared to him to be sacrilege. But faith in Christ is more a matter for the heart than the head. I am inclined to agree with Karl Rahner, who, exasperated by an interviewer's quest for a categorical answer to a question of doctrine, replied: 'Listen, I don't believe in God because I have worked out everything to the satisfaction of my mind. I continue to believe in God because I pray every day'.[1]

Conclusion

I end this postscript where it began, in Isières, remembering my comrades who are buried there. What a short life compared with mine. When I ask myself, how do I express thanks for having been spared, it is not only by thinking of some happy moment or satisfactory state of affairs which has come my way. I also remind myself that each day 'life is hanging in the balance' and that 'merely being alive is a gift of God'. I am quoting Rabbi Jonathan Sachs. He had been in Israel during the Gulf War and the experience of air raids had made him aware as never before, that the celebration of Rosh Hashanah, the Jewish New Year, is a reminder of that basic truth. 'Only when we know how fragile life is can we become self-

---

[1] Cited by M. P. Gallagher, *Free to Believe*, Darton, Longman and Todd, 1996 edition, p. 94.

conscious about it and learn to make a blessing over it.' Jews, because of their history, are particularly thankful that they still survive, but are we not all sometimes moved to believe that 'merely being alive' is a gift from God? So I thank God for the extension of my life, granted not just on 19 May 1940, but on every subsequent day and for bringing me under his wing.